Christianity Lost
What does it really mean to be a Christian?

H. NIGEL KASSEMBE

Copyright © 2017 H. Nigel Kassembe
All Rights Reserved
No part of this book may be used or reproduced in any manner whatsoever without written permission except in the case of brief quotations embodied in critical articles and reviews.

Request for information should be addressed to: Christianitylost@gmail.com

All Scripture quotations are from the King James Version.
ISBN: 0984542841
ISBN 13: 9780984542840

Matthew 16:24-28 (KJV)
"Then said Jesus unto his disciples, **If any *man* will come after me, let him deny himself, and take up his cross, and follow me.
For whosoever will save his life shall lose it: and whosoever will lose his life for my sake shall find it.
For what is a man profited, if he shall gain the whole world, and lose his own soul? or what shall a man give in exchange for his soul?
For the Son of man shall come in the glory of his Father with his angels; and then he shall reward every man according to his works.
Verily I say unto you, There be some standing here, which shall not taste of death, till they see the Son of man coming in his kingdom."

This book is dedicated to my brother J.D. and his beautiful family.
Love you guys!!!

Matthew 11:25-30 (KJV)

"At that time Jesus answered and said, **I thank thee, O Father, Lord of heaven and earth, because thou hast hid these things from the wise and prudent, and hast revealed them unto babes.**

Even so, Father: for so it seemed good in thy sight.

All things are delivered unto me of my Father: and no man knoweth the Son, but the Father; neither knoweth any man the Father, save the Son, and *he* **to whomsoever the Son will reveal** *him.*

Come unto me, all *ye* **that labour and are heavy laden, and I will give you rest.**

Take my yoke upon you, and learn of me; for I am meek and lowly in heart: and ye shall find rest unto your souls.

For my yoke *is* **easy, and my burden is light."**

CONTENTS

Introduction   xiii

1   The Bible   1
2   The Ten Commandments   18
3   Fornication   38
4   Doctrine   48
5   Speaking In Tongues   74
6   Gospel Music   122
7   Homosexuality   129
8   Christmas & Easter   146
9   Follow Me   177

Matthew 28:18-20 (KJV)

"And Jesus came and spake unto them, saying, **All power is given unto me in heaven and in earth.**
Go ye therefore, and teach all nations, baptizing them in the name of the Father, and of the Son, and of the Holy Ghost:
Teaching them to observe all things whatsoever I have commanded you: and, lo, I am with you alway, *even* unto the end of the world. Amen."

INTRODUCTION

My grandfather was a Reverend, I never really got a chance to know him that well, but what I remember about him is that, he seemed to always have a Bible with him. And I remember how he always seemed to be either praying or sitting quietly somewhere reading the Bible. And I used to wonder to myself, why is he always reading the Bible, because I mean, him being a Reverend, and also him being as old as he was, I figured he must have already finished reading the whole Bible back and forth probably a whole bunch of times already, you know what I mean!?

I also remember watching my grandfather on the pulpit preaching a few times, which I thought was pretty cool. I also admired his coolness, as he stood up there on the pulpit and told people about the Word of God. And as he preached, I remember looking around the room and seeing how people watched and listened to him attentively, as not wanting to miss any words. And I remember how majestic he looked, with his white robe perfectly clinging to his body, as he moved around speaking. I was around 6 or 7 years old at the time, so I wasn't really understanding what he was talking about, but it did spark my interest about God, and about Heaven and Hell (which seemed to be the focus of most of his sermons).

I never really was around my grandfather that much when I was younger, but the few times I was around him I enjoyed watching him pray and read his Bible faithfully. Also, I didn't really grow up in religious households, so I was always happy when Sundays came around and I got a chance to go to Sunday school and hear about God, and sing some songs about God, and also enjoy some of those delicious breakfast they used to serve for us kids, lol.

I never really had that many questions about God when I was little, I just loved going to Sunday school, sing some songs and try to learn how to avoid going to hell, you know what I mean!? But, when I turned about 10 years old, all of a sudden all these questions about God and about Christianity started occupying my mind heavily. I remember this one time, when I was around 10 or 11 years old, I remember sitting on the front porch of our house with a guy neighbor of ours (whom I used to help carry lamps to the market for his business, and this was in the early 80s in Tanzania Africa, where I was born), I remember sitting there asking him a whole bunch of questions about God and about Christianity. He did his best to answer most of my 10 year old questions, but mostly I remember him just saying that I will understand better and or more when I get older. And so ever since then, I have been on a slow grind to my understanding of God and Christianity. And the reason why I say "slow grind" is because it has taken me almost 30 years (I'm 42 years old now), to really feel like I have finally come to the real understanding about God and about what it really means to be a Christian. And the reason why it has taken me this long is because (and I've just come to realize this in the last few years, of why it took me so long), I never really actively searched out the Bible and pray for the understanding of what the verses really meant. And the funny thing is, even though I used to go to church and Bible study religiously when I was younger (I don't go to church much anymore, for a variety of reasons, in which I will be discussing some of them in the upcoming chapters in the book), I find that my spiritual growth has actually grown by leaps and bounds ever since I stopped going to church and actually started to actively search out the Bible for and by myself.

Now, there's nothing wrong with going to church and Bible study, and actually Bible study is probably the most important part of going to church, because that's usually where you really get a chance to study the verses, you know, where you actually get a chance to take each verse and break it down and debate and or discuss what the real meaning of the verses are. And so yeah, there's nothing wrong with going to church, I used to enjoy it (and I still do, whenever I do go, but I'm not a regular), but for some reason I always tended to fall asleep during service (as a youth), in which to this day I still contend to those being some of my best sleep ever, because I always woke up feeling extra refreshed, you know what I mean, can somebody say Amen, ha ha ha ha ha!

But yeah, anyway, what I have come to realize is that, even though the churches do their best to teach the Bible and give a person a good foundation as a Christian, the churches alone cannot foster your one on one spiritual relationship with the Lord, to where you really start to understand and start to live your life by the example that Jesus tried to teach us, in which we failed to understand when He was alive on earth physically with us (about 2000 years ago), and we are still failing to understand what He is trying to teach us right now (with the Bible, especially the New Testament), on what it really means to be a Christian. Now, when I say He has "tried to teach us", it by no means mean that He has failed, oh no, not at all, He has succeeded in his part (by example and by Word), but it is us who have failed and are continuing to fail more and more every day, as Christian people as a whole. And the reason why I say we continue to fail is because, from about 2000 years ago to today, we as Christians as a group, we have failed to live up to what the Bible demands of us. For example; we have failed to feed the hungry and cloth the poor (KJV- EZEKIEL 18:16; **"but hath given his bread to the hungry, and hath covered the naked with a garment"**), we have failed to shelter the homeless and to visit the sick (KJV- MATTHEW 25:35-36; **"I was a stranger, and ye took me in: I was sick, and ye visited me"**), we have failed to love our neighbors as we love ourselves (KJV- MARK 12:31; **"Thou shalt love thy neighbor as thyself"**), we have failed to not fornicate (KJV- 1 THESSALONIANS 4:3; **"For this is the will of God, even your sanctification, that ye should abstain from fornication"**), we have failed to not commit adultery (KJV- HEBREWS 13:4; **"Marriage is honourable in all, and the bed undefiled: but whoremongers and adulterers God will judge"**), we have failed to Love the Lord our God first (KJV- MARK 12:30; **"And thou shalt love the Lord thy God with all thy heart, and with all thy soul, and with all thy mind, and with all thy strength"**), we have failed not to be war mongers (KJV- JAMES 4:1-2; **"From whence come wars and fightings among you? come they not hence, even of your lusts that war in your members? Ye lust, and have not: ye kill, and desire to have, and cannot obtain: ye fight and war, yet ye have not, because ye ask not"**), we have failed to be the peace makers (KJV- MATTHEW 5:9; **"Blessed *are* the peacemakers: for they shall be called the children of God"**), we have failed to not speak falsely against one another

(KJV- PROVERBS 12:17; **"*He that* speaketh truth sheweth forth righteousness: but a false witness deceit"**), and so on and so on!

I mean, to be a Christian is not an easy task, especially if you really understand what it really means to be a Christian, and therefor accept and try to live by the examples of the teachings of Jesus Christ, who is the basis of Christianity. And this is the main reason why I decided to write this book, and it's because we are failing my fellow Christians, we are really failing in our understanding of what being a Christian is all about. And so, what I really want to do with this book is, I want to dig into the Bible and search out the scriptures and see what they have to tell us on what being a Christian is all about, and tell us what the Bible demands from us as followers of Jesus Christ.

Now, before we get started in searching the scriptures, I just want to say that, I by no means confess to being a Bible scholar, meaning, I am not a Preacher, I am not a Pastor, I am not a Minister, and so on, no, nothing like that (as we understand what these titles are supposed to mean in practical terms). And also, I have never been to any Divinity, Seminary, and or any other Bible training Institutions for that matter. I am just an average Joe who loves the Lord and strives to be a better Christian. And so all the statements and or answers that I will be providing will be coming straight from my understanding of what the scriptures are saying, and I will be doing this by praying and asking God to open my spiritual eyes, ears, mind and heart even more, so I can better discern the meaning of the verses with truth and pure understanding.

And so I want to thank you in advance for joining me in this Bible study (as I like to call it), as I search out the scriptures and try to explain and or Awaken the real understanding of what being a Christian is all about, so we Christians can Wake Up (in these End Days) and start to practice our Christianity with sincere hearts, minds and spirit, as we praise and thank the Lord for His mercy and for His gift of Salvation through His son Jesus Christ, who is our Lord and Savior. Amen!

1

THE BIBLE

The Bible is a very impressive book, I mean, the level of meticulousness that went into putting it together is very impressive. I mean, not only is it impressive in how the books, chapters and verses are arranged, but it is also very impressive on how it was written, I mean, from Genesis to Revelations, and how the wording, the sentence structure, and the details, including names, dates, cultural and historical backgrounds of key places and people that the Bible talks about, like; Jesus, Moses, Abraham and countless others, is very impressive. And to think about the fact that the Bible was only really put together (in its modern form) about 500 years ago, and for it to have perfect harmony from book to book, chapter to chapter, and verse to verse, that's very impressive!

And this is why the Bible has to definitely have been inspired by God, you know what I mean!? Because I mean, for the writers of the Bible to be able to tell the stories with such detail, and for the people who actually put the Bible together to be able to organize it in such a way that it flows in perfect order from beginning to end, notwithstanding the centuries that had passed since the writing took place, and when the modern Bible was actually put together, this leaves no question in my mind that Divine intervention had to play a huge part in the formation of the Bible. It is truly amazing, the Bible is just so amazing to me, what a blessing! And this is why they call the Bible "the Greatest Book ever written," because it's just so impressive!

The Bible is comprised of two parts; **The Old Testament** (Moses's time) and **The New Testament** (Jesus's time), and each part has numerous books in it that makes up the part. The Old Testament has 46 books in it, and the New Testament has 27 books in it, and all these books together make up the one Bible. Now, let's check out these two parts of the Bible and see what they are all about!

The Old Testament

The Old Testament is pretty much about letting us know that God created the world and everything in it, including us humans. It also tells us not only how and why he created us, but also what He expected of us, which is for us to love Him as He loves us, so we can reign on earth forever as His greatest creation, made in His own image. Now, let's open up the Bible and see what The Old Testament actually says, in its own words about how and why God created us, and what He expected from us!

(KJV-Genesis 1:1-11; **"In the beginning God created the heaven and the earth. And the earth was without form, and void; and darkness was upon the face of the deep. And the Spirit of God moved upon the face of the waters. And God said, Let there be light: and there was light. And God saw the light, that it was good: and God divided the light from the darkness. And God called the light Day, and the darkness he called Night. And the evening and the morning were the first day. And God said, Let there be a firmament in the midst of the waters, and let it divide the waters from the waters. And God made the firmament, and divided the waters which were under the firmament from the waters which were above the firmament: and it was so. And God called the firmament Heaven. And the evening and the morning were the second day. And God said, Let the waters under the heaven be gathered together unto one place, and let the dry land appear: and it was so. And God called the dry land Earth; and the gathering together of the waters called he Seas: and God** saw that it was good. And God said, Let the earth bring forth grass, the herb yielding seed, and the fruit tree yielding fruit after his kind, whose seed is in itself, upon the earth: and it was so").

So as you can see, God created the world, no Big Bang stuff here, which makes no sense to me, because I mean, how do you get something out of nothing, which is what the Big Bang theory people want us to believe, I mean, that's like believing 0+0=1, which is elementary stuff, so please, give me a break, if you don't believe in God, just say you don't know how the world came to be, but enough with the Big Bang stuff, it insults some of our intelligence. Anyway, let's continue!

(KJV-Genesis 1:26 & 2:7; **"And God said, Let us make man in our image, after our likeness: and let them have dominion over the fish of the sea, and over the fowl of the air, and over the cattle, and over all the earth, and over every creeping thing that creepeth upon the earth. And the LORD God formed man** *of* **the dust of the ground, and breathed into his nostrils the breath of life; and man became a living soul"**).

Now, as you can see, God created humans, humans didn't evolve from no monkeys (as the evolution people try to tell us, come on give me a break with all these elementary scientific theories). So, now we know that God created us, now let's find out why He created us, let's read some more!

(KJV-Genesis 1:27-28; **"So God created man in his** *own* **image, in the image of God created he him; male and female created he them. And God blessed them, and God said unto them, Be fruitful, and multiply, and replenish the earth, and subdue it: and have dominion over the fish of the sea, and over the fowl of the air, and over every living thing that moveth upon the earth"**).

So, one of the reasons why God created humans is so we could reign over the earth, you know, control the earth and the animals and every other living thing in it. But there's another reason we were created, let's read some more!

(KJV- Genesis 17:7; **"And I will establish my covenant between me and thee and thy seed after thee in their generations for an everlasting covenant, to be a God unto thee, and to thy seed after thee"**).

So, as you can see, the other reason why God created us is so we could enjoy everlasting life with Him, with Him being our God, and us being His children. For God wanted to share His love with us, and for us to love Him back (with free will, not forced). But, as you already know, we started sinning and going against Gods' Will right of the jump, you know, not long after we were created and placed in the Garden of Eden, you know, from Adam and Eve. Let's read some more and see what the Bible says about this!

(KJV- Genesis 2:15-17; **"And the LORD God took the man, and put him into the garden of Eden to dress it and to keep it. And the LORD God commanded the man, saying, Of every tree of the garden thou mayest freely eat: But of the tree of the knowledge of good and evil, thou shalt not eat of it: for in the day that thou eatest thereof thou shalt surely die"**).

Now, the reason why God did not want us to gain knowledge of good and evil is because, he knew that our flesh would most likely lead us into doing more evil than into doing good. And this is because our flesh is weak, you know, making us more susceptible into being misled into living wicked lifestyles than righteous ones, you know what I mean. And the reason why we are so easily misled into living wicked lifestyles than righteous ones is because, us as humans, we don't really poses total control over our mind, body and spirit, meaning, we don't really have the strength to totally fight off wicked temptations, you know, like; lying, stealing, cheating, killing, fornicating, adultery, and so on and so on! And this is why we need God in our lives, you know, to give us that extra strength to fight off a bunch of these temptations that the Devil continuously tries to get us into, you know what I mean!?

So yeah, we were created to have everlasting life with God (right here on earth), but after Adam and Eve disobeyed God by eating that apple, God took the everlasting life (right here on earth), away from us. Let's read a little bit about it!

(KJV-Genesis 3:1-6; **"Now the serpent was more subtil than any beast of the field which the LORD God had made. And he said unto the woman, Yea, hath God said, Ye shall not eat of every tree of the garden? And the woman said unto the serpent, We may eat of the fruit of the trees of the garden: But of the fruit of the tree which *is* in the midst of the garden, God hath said, Ye shall not eat of it, neither shall ye touch it, lest ye die. And the serpent said unto the woman, Ye shall not surely die: For God doth know that in the day ye eat thereof, then your eyes shall be opened, and ye shall be as gods, knowing good and evil. And when the woman saw that the tree *was* good for food, and that it *was* pleasant to the eyes, and a tree to be desired to make *one* wise, she took of the fruit thereof, and did eat, and gave also unto her husband with her; and he did eat"**).

It's amazing how easy it seems to be for the Devil to deceive us, right!? It's almost like he knows our weaknesses and he works over time to use them to get us to commit sins. I mean it's crazy, but it's almost like he's on our left shoulder screaming louder for us to do bad than the angel that is supposed to be on our right shoulder trying to get us to do good, you know what I mean!? And it's almost interesting how the Devil used Eve to get Adam to sin, you know, he used the woman to get the man to sin. And the reason why he used Eve to get Adam to sin is because, he knew that Adam would not suspect his wife to trick him into sinning, you know, cause that's his wife, he trust her, he has no reason to think that she will deceive him. So it's like, the Devil knew that if he went to Adam first, most likely than not Adam would tell him to go to hell, leave him and his wife alone, you know, he's not about to disobey God by eating to apple and gaining wisdom, forget wisdom, he's got his wife, and he's got a garden full of other fruits he can eat, he's good to go, he don't need nothing else.

And the reason why I say this is because, usually guys are not that curious about stuff, you know, usually guys just wanna go to work and come back home and be fruitful and multiply with their woman and just chill and relax, you know what I mean!? But on the other hand, woman tend to be a little bit more curious about stuff than guys, you know, woman just can't help it but wanna know stuff, even if that stuff concerns them or not, and even if that stuff won't really add anything positive to their own life, woman just can't help it, they just gotta know it. And this is why woman tend to do a lot of gossip and stuff like that, you know, because they just so curious about anything and everything that they end up being on and or exposing other people's business that they might not even have real knowledge about it, you know what I mean!?

And so anyway, yeah, Eve really didn't have much of a choice but to eat the apple, because the thought of gaining wisdom and knowing stuff was just too much for her to pass up. And so she went ahead and ate the apple, and of course gave it to her trusting husband to eat some also, which he did, and right away he realized she had deceived him, but she didn't really meant to, she was just deceived herself by the Devil, who used her curiosity weakness to cause both of them to disobey God. And this is where man's sinning against God began, and this is when man lost their everlasting life here on earth. Let's read some more and see what the Bible says about this!

(KJV-Genesis 3:22-24; **"And the LORD God said, Behold, the man is become as one of us, to know good and evil: and now, lest he put forth his hand, and take also of the tree of life, and eat, and live for ever: Therefore the LORD God sent him forth from the garden of Eden, to till the ground from whence he was taken. So he drove out the man; and he placed at the east of the garden of Eden Cherubims, and a flaming sword which turned every way, to keep the way of the tree of life"**).

So, as you can see, we were supposed to have everlasting life right here on earth, but because of our sinning, God took that away from us, but He did provide for another way for us to gain everlasting life, not here on earth though, but in Heaving, as we'll see when we get to the New Testament. And so after God removed Adam and Eve from the Garden of Eden, He still showed them love and told them to go be fruitful and multiply, which is exactly what they did. But, not long after Adam and Eve had their first two sons (Cane and Abel), the first son killed the second son, you know, Cane killed Abel. And why did Cane kill Abel, and it's all because Cane was jealous that God seemed to favor Abel more than himself. I mean it's crazy, but Cane actually killed his own brother because of jealousy, is that crazy or what! But as we all know, jealousy is another one of man's weaknesses, I'm I right or wrong!?

And actually, jealousy can actually be one of man's biggest weaknesses, and the reason I say this is because, jealousy can easy turn into hate, and hate is one of the worst human traits, because it can easily turn people into monsters, you know, making them capable of doing unspeakable acts of evilness to other people and or nations. And so, this is why Cane killed Abel, and it was because his jealousy had turned into hate towards his brother. Now, it's amazing how even though God cursed Cane for killing his brother, God still showed Cane favor by putting a mark on him for protection so he Cane won't be killed. Let's read the Bible and see what it says on this part!

(JKV-Genesis 4:1-17; **"And Adam knew Eve his wife; and she conceived, and bare Cain, and said, I have gotten a man from the LORD. And she again bare his brother Abel. And Abel was a keeper of sheep, but Cain was a tiller of the ground. And in process of time it came to pass, that Cain brought of the fruit of the ground an offering unto the LORD. And Abel, he also brought of the firstlings of his flock and of the fat thereof. And the LORD had respect unto Abel and to his offering: But unto Cain and to his offering he had not respect. And Cain was very wroth, and his countenance fell.**

And the LORD said unto Cain, Why art thou wroth? and why is thy countenance fallen? If thou doest well, shalt thou not be accepted? and if thou doest not well, sin lieth at the door. And unto thee *shall be* his desire, and thou shalt rule over him.

And Cain talked with Abel his brother: and it came to pass, when they were in the field, that Cain rose up against Abel his brother, and slew him. And the LORD said unto Cain, Where *is* Abel thy brother? And he said, I know not: *Am* I my brother's keeper? And he said, What hast thou done? the voice of thy brother's blood crieth unto me from the ground. And now *art* thou cursed from the earth, which hath opened her mouth to receive thy brother's blood from thy hand; When thou tillest the ground, it shall not henceforth yield unto thee her strength; a fugitive and a vagabond shalt thou be in the earth.

And Cain said unto the LORD, My punishment *is* greater than I can bear. Behold, thou hast driven me out this day from the face of the earth; and from thy face shall I be hid; and I shall be a fugitive and a vagabond in the earth; and it shall come to pass, *that* every one that findeth me shall slay me. And the LORD said unto him, Therefore whosoever slayeth Cain, vengeance shall be taken on him sevenfold. And the LORD set a mark upon Cain, lest any finding him should kill him. And Cain went out from the presence of the LORD, and dwelt in the land of Nod, on the east of Eden. And Cain knew his wife; and she conceived, and bare Enoch: and he builded a city, and called the name of the city, after the name of his son, Enoch").

Ok, so, what this Cane and Abel story shows us is that, God is a merciful God, because even though Cane committed one of the worst sins (murder), God still loved him enough to allow him to be fruitful and multiply and be prosperous (built his own city). Now, the verses don't tell us if Cane repented of his sin, but he did complain to God that his punishment was greater than he could bear, and God showed him mercy by putting a mark of protection on him. And so, stories like this, where man commit sins and God continue to show mercy are plentiful in the Old Testament. And this is what the Old Testament is all about, it's about showing and or telling us how sinful us human beings really are that we couldn't Save ourselves if we wanted to, you know what I mean? I mean, I don't know what it is, but it's like our human nature for some reason tends to so easily gravitate towards wickedness than towards righteousness. And this is the reason why God had to Save us himself (by Grace), you know, by sending us a savior (himself in human form) Jesus Christ, so that all we gotta do is repent of our sins and accept Jesus as our Lord and Savior, and that's it, Salvation is ours!

And so as you can see, God really does have a soft spot for us humans, because I mean, for him to keep giving us chances after chances after chances, it only shows how much is love for us really is. And so this is what the Old Testament is trying to show us, and that is, how much God really loves us, and how we are prone to wickedness. And the interesting thing is, God was actually very active in the affairs of man back in the Bible days. I mean, plenty of times, God would actually come down and speak to chosen individuals (who were righteous in His eyes) and tell them how unhappy He is about the wickedness that's going on, and also He would tell them to warn the people that if they don't stop with their wicked ways God might just come down and destroy their whole nation. And this is one of the reasons why there seems to be a lot of wars in the Bible, and it's because when the wickedness of a nation got to be too much for God to ignore, He would usually raise up an army to go and destroy and kill all the people in that wicked nation. And a few times God actually did the destroying Himself, you know, like in Noah's time with the flood. Let's read some of this part of the story in the Bible!

(KJV-Genesis 6:5-14, 17-22; **"And GOD saw that the wickedness of man *was* great in the earth, and *that* every imagination of the thoughts of his heart *was* only evil continually. And it repented the LORD that he had made man on the earth, and it grieved him at his heart. And the LORD said, I will destroy man whom I have created** from the face of the earth; both man, and beast, and the creeping thing, and the fowls of the air; for it repenteth me that I have made them. But Noah found grace in the eyes of the LORD. These *are* the generations of Noah: Noah was a just man *and* perfect in his generations, *and* Noah walked with God. And Noah begat three sons, Shem, Ham, and Japheth. The earth also was corrupt before God, and the earth was filled with violence. And God looked upon the earth, and, behold, it was corrupt; for all flesh had corrupted his way upon the earth. And God said unto Noah, The end of all flesh is come before me; for the earth is filled with violence through them; and, behold, I will destroy them with the earth. Make thee an ark of gopher wood; rooms shalt thou make in the ark, and shalt pitch it within and without with pitch").

So God had had enough with the wickedness that was taking place in the world and was ready to destroy every living thing in it. But, God did found one man who was righteous in His sight (Noah), and God decided to save him. Let's read some more!

(KJV-Genesis 7:4-7, 12, 19-24; **"And the LORD said unto Noah, Come thou and all thy house into the ark; for thee have I seen righteous before me in this generation. For yet seven days, and I will cause it to rain upon the earth forty days and forty nights; and every living substance that I have made will I destroy from off the face of the earth. And Noah did according unto all that the LORD commanded him. And Noah *was* six hundred years old when the flood of waters was upon the earth. And Noah went in, and his sons, and his wife, and his sons' wives with him, into the ark, because of the waters of the flood. And the rain was upon the earth forty days and forty nights. And the waters prevailed exceedingly upon the earth; and all the high hills, that *were* under the whole heaven, were covered. Fifteen cubits upward did the waters prevail; and the mountains were covered. And all flesh died that moved upon the earth, both of fowl, and of cattle, and of beast, and of every creeping thing that creepeth** upon the earth, and every man: All in whose nostrils *was* the breath of life, of all that *was* in the dry *land*, died. And every living substance was destroyed which was upon the face of the ground, both man, and cattle, and the creeping things, and the fowl of the heaven; and they were destroyed from the earth: and Noah only remained *alive*, and they that *were* with him in the ark. And the waters prevailed upon the earth an hundred and fifty days").

So God caused it to rain for forty days and forty nights, and the water covered everything, including hills and mountains, and so every living thing on earth died, except for Noah and his family and the animals that went in the Ark with him. Let's read some more!

(KJV-Genesis 8:1-22 & 9:1 **"And God remembered Noah, and every living thing, and all the cattle that *was* with him in the ark: and God made a wind to pass over the earth, and the waters asswaged; The fountains also of the deep and the windows of heaven were stopped, and the rain from heaven was restrained; And the waters returned from off the earth continually: and after the end of the hundred and fifty days the waters were abated. And the ark rested in the seventh month, on the seventeenth day of the month, upon the mountains of Ararat. And the waters decreased continually until the tenth month: in the tenth *month*, on the first *day* of the month, were the tops of the mountains seen.**

And it came to pass at the end of forty days, that Noah opened the window of the ark which he had made: And he sent forth a raven, which went forth to and fro, until the waters were dried up from off the earth. Also he sent forth a dove from him, to see if the waters were abated from off the face of the ground: But the dove found no rest for the sole of her foot, and she returned unto him into the ark, for the waters *were* on the face of the whole earth: then he put forth his hand, and took her, and pulled her in unto him into the ark. And he stayed yet other seven days; and again he sent forth the dove out

of the ark; And the dove came in to him in the evening; and, lo, in her mouth *was* an olive leaf pluckt off: so Noah knew that the waters were abated from off the earth. And he stayed yet other seven days; and sent forth the dove; which returned not again unto him any more.

And it came to pass in the six hundredth and first year, in the first *month*, the first *day* of the month, the waters were dried up from off the earth: and Noah removed the covering of the ark, and looked, and, behold, the face of the ground was dry. And in the second month, on the seven and twentieth day of the month, was the earth dried. And God spake unto Noah, saying, Go forth of the ark, thou, and thy wife, and thy sons, and thy sons' wives with thee. Bring forth with thee every living thing that *is* with thee, of all flesh, *both* of fowl, and of cattle, and of every creeping thing that creepeth upon the earth; that they may breed abundantly in the earth, and be fruitful, and multiply upon the earth.

And Noah went forth, and his sons, and his wife, and his sons' wives with him: Every beast, every creeping thing, and every fowl, *and* whatsoever creepeth upon the earth, after their kinds, went forth out of the ark. And Noah built an altar unto the LORD; and took of every clean beast, and of every clean fowl, and offered burnt offerings on the altar. And the LORD smelled a sweet savour; and the LORD said in his heart, I will not again curse the ground any more for man's sake; for the imagination of man's heart *is* evil from his youth; neither will I again smite any more every thing living, as I have done. While the earth remaineth, seedtime and harvest, and cold and heat, and summer and winter, and day and night shall not cease. And God blessed Noah and his sons, and said unto them, Be fruitful, and multiply, and replenish the earth").

So, God caused a flood to happen, which killed every living thing on earth except for Noah and his family, which God preserved, and in which He used to start a new generation (replenish the earth). Also, did you notice how bad God felt about destroying every living thing on earth, to the point where He said he will never do it again, as long as the earth is still here (until judgment day). And so, this is what the Old Testament is all about, it's about showing us how wicked human beings have a tendency to be ("**for the imagination of man's heart *is* evil from his youth"**), making it hard for us to become righteous by our own will. And so this is also why God gave us the New Testament, and it's so He himself can help us become righteous, by Him himself dwelling inside of us (through the Holy Ghost), after we repent of our sins and accept Jesus Christ us our Lord and Savior. Now, there's a lot more stories in the Old Testament about God's love and mercy for us as we continue to be wicked (which I encourage everyone to take their time and read it, because it's good for not only increasing our knowledge of the Old Testament, but it's also good for building our understand of the Bible as a whole), but for now I want us to move on to the New Testament and see what it's all about!

The New Testament

The New Testament is pretty much about telling us the good news of how God has made a way for us to receive salvation, and has done so by Grace, meaning it's free, all we have to do is accept it! And so, unlike the Old Testament, where God kept giving us laws after laws so that we could obey and become righteous, in the New Testament God made it very simple for us to become righteous and obtain salvation, and that is by us repenting of our sins and accepting Jesus Christ as our Lord and Savior (who was pretty much God Himself in human form, when He was here with us on earth before He died and went back to Heaven). The New Testament is also about telling us and or warning us about what will happen to those who don't receive salvation (aka those who don't make it to Heaven) when judgement day comes. Ok, let's open up The New Testament and read some and see what it has to tell us!

(KJV-John 1:1-18; **"In the beginning was the Word, and the Word was with God, and the Word was God. The same was in the beginning** with God. All things were made by him; and without him was not any thing made that was made. In him was life; and the life was the light of men. And the light shineth in darkness; and the darkness comprehended it not. There was a man sent from God, whose name *was* John. The same came for a witness, to bear witness of the Light, that all *men* through him might believe. He was not that Light, but *was sent* to bear witness of that Light. *That* was the true Light, which lighteth every man that cometh into the world. He was in the world, and the world was made by him, and the world knew him not. He came unto his own, and his own received him not. But as many as received him, to them gave he power to become the sons of God, *even* to them that believe on his name: Which were born, not of blood, nor of the will of the flesh, nor of the will of man, but of God.

And the Word was made flesh, and dwelt among us, (and we beheld his glory, the glory as of the only begotten of the Father,) full of grace and truth. John bare witness of him, and cried, saying, This was he of whom I spake, He that cometh after me is preferred before me: for he was before me. And of his fulness have all we received, and grace for grace. For the law was given by Moses, *but* grace and truth came by Jesus Christ. No man hath seen God at any time; the only begotten Son, which is in the bosom of the Father, he hath declared *him").*

Ok so, this scripture tells us about how God himself came down and not only gave us Salvation through Grace (**"And of his fulness have all we received, and grace for grace"**), but it tells us that God actually lived among us (**"He was in the world, and the world was made by him, and the world knew him not"**). So, many people did not believe that He was actually God in flesh (**"He came unto his own, and his own received him not"**), but many others did believe, and right away they were Saved (**"But as many as received him, to them gave he power to become the sons of God, *even* to them that believe on his name"**). This scripture also tells us that we are no longer Saved by the Law (**"For the law was given by Moses"), but we are now Saved by Grace (***"but grace and truth came by Jesus Christ"***).

Now, it's amazing how God came on earth as flesh, you know, in human form, through a human being (Mary), as Jesus Christ (His son). Let's read a little bit about this part in the bible!

(KJV-Matthew 1:18-25; **"Now the birth of Jesus Christ was on this wise: When as his mother Mary was espoused to Joseph, before they came together, she was found with child of the Holy Ghost. Then Joseph her husband, being a just *man*, and not willing to make her a publick example, was minded to put her away privily. But while he thought on these things, behold, the angel of the Lord appeared unto him in a dream, saying, Joseph, thou son of David, fear not to take unto thee Mary thy wife: for that which is conceived in her is of the Holy Ghost. And she shall bring forth a son, and thou shalt call his name JESUS: for he shall save his people from their sins. Now all this was done, that it might be fulfilled which was spoken of the Lord by the prophet, saying, Behold, a virgin shall be with child, and shall bring forth a son, and they shall call his name Emmanuel, which being interpreted is, God with us. Then Joseph being raised from sleep did as the angel of the Lord had bidden him, and took unto him his wife: And knew her not till she had brought forth her firstborn son: and he called his name JESUS"**).

It's amazing isn't it, how God actually went through the whole process of being born from a human! And I mean, He actually went through the whole process of growing up, you know, from a baby to a grown up. Now, I wonder why there's pretty much no details about Him as a kid, but I'm guessing it's probably because Mary and Joseph just raised Him as a normal kid, so no one saw no reason to document His younger days. But, wouldn't it had been nice if there was a record of His youth, you know, just so we can see if He was just like other kids in the neighborhood and went out and played with the other kids, or if He just pretty much kept to Himself and just waited for the age, day and hour to come so He could finally start His ministry and work on fulfilling His mission that He came to do, you know what I mean!?

But so, yeah anyway, it's amazing how God chose to come as flesh through a regular birth, because I mean, if He wanted to, He could have just all of a sudden appear on earth as a human being just like that, you know, like out of nowhere, you know what I mean!? And I think the reason why He came to earth through birth is because, I think He wanted to have a earthly background story so as to make it easier for the people to relate to Him, you know, make it easier for the people to feel comfortable around Him, you know, like He's just like one of them, you know, because not only have them seen Him growing up, but they know who His parents are, you know what I mean!? And so, it's like, instead of people trying to figure out who He is and or where He came from, they will pretty much already know, you know, the carpenter's son from Nazareth. Now, this is also one the reasons a lot of the people had a hard time believing that He was indeed the Messiah, and it's because a lot of them had known Him from His youth, so they had a hard time believing that that little boy that was probably out there playing around with the other little kids is actually the Savior Himself, you know what I mean!?

But, I think it was genius for God to come to earth through a regular birth, and the reason I say this is because, God did not want to just impose His Will on us, you know, He did not want us to accept Him and His gift of Salvation for us (through Christ) by force and or intimidation. And what I mean is, God doesn't want us to accept His gift of Salvation because we fear Him, oh no, He wants us to accept His gift of Salvation because we Love Him. And this is why Jesus was so humble in His teaching and on how He carried Himself, and it's because He did not want to intimidate the people into believing in Him, oh no, He wanted His actions and words to be the factor of people believing in Him. But, His humbleness was probably one of the reasons why a lot of people had a hard time believing that He was actually the Messiah, you know, because they were probably expecting the Messiah to come acting and or looking all Majestic and stuff, you know what I mean!? I mean, they were probably expecting someone who had more of a forceful personality, you know, and or probably they were looking for someone who would be surrounded by priests and or other clergy man. But, nah, Jesus came very humble, I mean, He came so humble that even the priests and other religious people at the time had a hard time recognizing Him, because you would think they would know better, right? And also on top of that, His disciples were just regular Joes, (mostly fisherman), I mean, how much more humble can humble get!

But, that's how God wanted it, He wants us to believe in Jesus Christ out of love and appreciation for the Salvation that He has made available for us freely, without any intimidation from Him, but by our free will and pure heart. And so, this is what The New Testament is all about, and it's about telling us that God has made a way for us to obtain Salvation freely (by Grace), and all we have to do is repent of our sins and believe that Jesus Christ is our Lord and Savior, that's it, simple, I think this is as simple as God could have made it! Now, The New Testament also talks about the consequences of not receiving Salvation, which is condemnation (aka going to Hell). So I encourage everyone to take their time and read **The New Testament** as well as **The Old Testament**, so your knowledge and understanding of the whole Bible can be greatly increased!

2

THE TEN COMMANDMENTS

If you are a Christian, most likely than not, you have heard of the **Ten Commandments**, which are the ten set of rules that God gave to Moses up at Mount Sinai, in which Moses was to teach them to the people so the people can know how to live a righteous life. And the Commandments were given not long after God had helped Moses get the people out of bondage from Pharaoh in Egypt. And the people were Jews, in which God had favored and had chosen as His people, in which He was gonna use to build a great righteous nation. But of course the Jews eventually started rebelling again and going back to their wicked ways, and that's why God kinda gave up on them and brought us the Messiah and commanded the disciples to take the message of the Bible to the Gentiles. But so anyway, let's check out the Ten Commandments and see what God wants us to not do, as a way for us to stay righteous.

1st Commandment

KJV-Exodus 20:3; **"Thou shalt have no other gods before me."**

I think this Commandment is pretty clear, God doesn't want us to have any other gods besides Him, that's plain and simple. But of course God had to give us this Commandment so that we truly understand that there's only one God and He is it. And the reason why God had to give this Commandment is because, the people in the Bible days had a habit of creating statues of all kinds and calling them their gods, and so God wanted to make sure they knew that there's only one God and He is it!

2nd **Commandment**

KJV-Exodus 20:4; **"Thou shalt not make unto thee any graven image, or any likeness** *of any thing* **that** *is* **in heaven above, or that** *is* **in the earth beneath, or that** *is* **in the water under the earth."**

I wonder how many Christians have really read this Commandment, and the reason why I say this is because, the Commandment is telling us not to make any images of anything that is likeness in Heaven, meaning, we should not make any pictures that are supposed to depict God and or Christ, but what do we do, we go ahead and make so many images that are supposed to depict Jesus Christ, you know, totally going against this Commandment. And this is one of the reasons why I decided to write this book, and it's because the more and more I read the Bible, the more and more I start to realize that we as Christians are not really practicing our Christianity as the Bible instruct us to. And the reason why we not practicing our Christianity the way the Bible wants us to is because, we really don't know what it really means to be a Christian. And the reason why we don't really know what it really means to be a Christian is because, we are not very good at reading the Bible, meaning, we are not very good at interpreting the scriptures, therefor we tend to go with the doctrine and or theology that we are accustomed to. And what I mean by accustomed to is, we tend to just follow what the custom of our denomination practices, you know, without checking the scriptures for ourselves to see if what we are practicing is actually Biblical or not. And the reason we tend not to deeply check the scriptures for ourselves is because, most people tend to actually be intimidated by the Bible, meaning, they are afraid that they will have a hard time understanding it, you know, they fear they won't do a good job discerning the meaning of the verses, you know, with all those thy, thou, shall, and etc, you know what I mean!? And so, for most people, they would rather just go to church and let the pastor tell them what the Bible is saying, you know, trusting that their pastor is truly anointed to better discern the scriptures. But this can greatly be a problem, because if people end up in a church where the pastor himself is not very good at discerning the scriptures, then you can easy end up in a situation where the people can be greatly mislead, you know, almost like the blind leading the blind, you know what I mean!?

And so, this is one of the reasons why I decided to write this book, and it's because I keep running into scriptures that totally contradict some of these church doctrines that some of our fellow Christians are practicing. And this is the reason why I called this book "Christianity Lost," and it's because it seems like to me that most of us Christians are just going through the motion of trying to be a good Christian by just following whatever the doctrine is of the church we belong to, and unfortunately for most Christians, their churches are not really teaching them and or are not really urging them to read the Bible for themselves, thereby most people are just left to practice their Christianity like robots, you know, just following, and hoping that their leaders won't mislead them.

But so anyway, back to the **2ⁿᵈ Commandment**, when I finally really read it, my mouth almost dropped to the floor with disbelief, of how millions of Christians seem to not understand it, and or, how millions of Christians seem to be ok with disobeying the Commandment, which states that, we should not be making any images of God or Jesus Christ. I mean, the Commandment is so plain, it's so simple, how could millions of Christians just not understand it, I mean, it says no images of Heaven or the likeness of it, which means, no images of the likeness of God or Jesus Christ. I mean it's crazy, I mean I just don't get it, I just don't understand how no one that is in the churches that are heavy into having images of Christ all up in their churches and or homes, I don't understand how no one has been able to read the second commandment and say, hold up, wait a minute, something is wrong here, we might have to re-examine the second commandment, because I think it's telling us not to have no images of God or Christ made. Because I mean, the Bible has been around for a little more than five hundred years, and so you would think that in that time frame surely someone (especially in the leadership position) would have discerned the true meaning of the second commandment and let others know of the error that their church has committed, and there for a correction of the practice of images can be banished from their tradition. But so, of course no one seems to have discovered the error, and what we have today is millions of Christians worshipping idols that are supposed to be the image of Christ. And the most popular idol is the white guy with blond hair with blue eye, you know the one, the one that looks like a pretty surfer dude from California, you know the one, right!? I mean it's crazy, people got this surfer looking dude dressed in robes with blond hair and blue eyes all up on their walls, thinking that that's how Jesus looks, so they go ahead and worship the image thinking that they are worshipping God but instead they are just worshipping a painting that someone won a prize for best drawing contest depicting Jesus. I mean it's crazy, and it's really sad at the same time, because these people have no idea that not only that those images are not Jesus, but that it's a sin to make images of Jesus. And it gets even sadder knowing that these people not only are not worshipping Christ with those images, but they are really worshipping idols, which is another sin, so you got double sinning going on with the images.

And so this is why God does not want us to make images of His or Jesus's likeness, it's because we not gonna be worshipping Him with the images, we pretty much just gonna be worshipping idols, thinking they are God, which they are not!

There's also a second part to this commandment, which says; **"Thou shalt not bow down thyself to them, nor serve them: for I the LORD thy God *am* a jealous God, visiting the iniquity of the fathers upon the children unto the third and fourth *generation* of them that hate me; And shewing mercy unto thousands of them that love me, and keep my commandments."** KJV-Exodus 20:5-6

Ok so, this part of the commandment is a continuation of the second commandment, where as in the first part God tells us not to make images of Him or Jesus, in this part of the commandment He's telling us not to bow down or worship the images. And notice how God says that He is a jealous God, and the reason why He says that is because He is proud of

His greatest creation, which is us humans, and He wants us to love Him as much as He loves us. And so it's like, by us worshipping other Gods, it's like us saying that we don't love Him (our creator). And that's why if you notice, He said, "He will visit iniquity to them that hate Him, and He will show mercy to them that love Him. And how do you love God? You love God by obeying His commandments. And this is what the third commandment is all about, you know, don't make any images of God or Jesus, and don't worship them!

3ᵗʰ **Commandment**

KJV-Exodus 20:7; **"Thou shalt not take the name of the LORD thy God in vain; for the LORD will not hold him guiltless that taketh his name in vain."**

Truth be told, this commandment kinda kicked my butt a little bit, as far as trying to discern it. And the reason why it kicked my butt is because, I was having a hard time trying to figure out whether "in vain" just meant not saying the word God in our everyday conversations (you know, like in saying "Oh my God", or saying something like "God damn it", you know, everyday phrases like that), or if "in vain" actually had a deeper meaning to it than just saying the word God in our casual expressions. And what I mean by casual is, using the word God in our everyday conversations that are not spiritual in manner, you know, using it casually instead of like in worship, praise, prayer or etc., you know, where God's name is used to glorify Him.

And so I had to sit with this commandment in my head for a few days, because I really felt like there must be a deeper meaning to it than just simply using the word God casually. Now, of course it's probably not a good idea to use the word God casually, because God is Holy, and using His name casually could easily be disrespectful and or even sinful, especially when used in vulgar conversations. But even with this being said, I still thought there was a deeper meaning to this commandment than just saying God casually, but I was having a hard time figuring out what that deeper meaning was. So I decided to go to the internet and see what others (who seem to have studied the Bible more than me) had to say about it, but I didn't find any answers that stood out to me, most of the people just thought it meant the simple use of God in everyday conversation and or in blasphemy, and others kinda went extra deep on it, you know, breaking down the history of the time and what the original meaning of the words "take in vain" might have meant in its original dialect and stuff (which kinda lost me, lol).

So I had to sit with this commandment in my head for a few more extra days and pray on it and wait for God to give me some clues to what its' real meaning is. Then one day the words "for granted" and "sincere" kept coming to my mind. So then I started thinking, ok, maybe "in vain" means not taking Gods name for granted, as in, we need to recognize the Holiness of God's name, and therefore, we should not take God's name as being not a big deal, and end up misusing it any which way how, without regard to its reverence and or without fear of it. Now, when I say misuse, I'm not just talking about the simple use of the word God, I'm really talking about using the word God in association with telling lies, deceit, and etc., and using God as a tool to booster your lies and etc., knowing that people will most likely believe you since you are swearing to God that what you are saying is the truth, even though you know that you are lying. And so in this scenario, you used God's name in vain, because you used God's name to lie, which means you used God's name for nothing ("in vain", which the dictionary defines it as meaning "for nothing" or "emptiness"), except for your own benefit, which is to make the people believe your lie.

Now, the other word that kept coming to me as I was thinking about this commandment is, "sincere". And so as I think of the word (sincere) in association with the words "in vain", what comes to mind is, this commandment is telling us that when we pray, worship, praise, preach and or etc., we have to make sure we are sincere about it, otherwise ore prayers, worship, praise, preaching, and or etc., will be for nothing, meaning it will be "in vain", because we are not sincere about it, almost like we just going through the motions, you know, faking it. And the reason why God gave us this commandment is because He doesn't want us to pretend to be holy, or pretend to be righteous, or pretend to be spiritual, you know, using God's name to make ourselves appear holy outwardly (to other people) but inside (in our hearts) we really not. And this is why in the book of John 4:23 (KJV) it says, **"But the hour cometh, and now is, when the true worshippers shall worship the Father in spirit and in truth: for the Father seeketh such to worship him."** Ok, so you see, God wants us to worship Him in spirit and in truth, meaning, no fakeness, because otherwise our worship will be "in vain", for nothing.

And so after I finally came to the conclusion that this commandment is telling us to; (1) not take God's name for granted, and (2) we have to be sincere about our worship and or etc., I went back on the internet to see if anybody else had a similar conclusion of this commandment as me. I didn't find exact conclusions, but I did find a few people that had conclusions that were kinda similar to mine in some parts. And one guy provided a few scriptures to back up his opinions of the commandment, and two of the scriptures stood out to me, so let's check them out real quick. The first one is; Jeremiah 14:14 (KJV), and it says, **"Then the LORD said unto me, The prophets prophesy lies in my name: I sent them not, neither have I commanded them, neither spake unto them: they prophesy unto you a false vision and divination, and a thing of nought, and the deceit of their heart"**. Ok, did you catch that, did you see how it says **"the prophets prophesy lies in my name"**, meaning, the preachers are telling the people lies, you know, like when they say something like; "God said this is your year to get that big house, that new car" and or etc., you know, when actually God didn't say no such thing, but the preachers just say that so as to appease their congregations, but it's a lie. And did you see how it says **"they prophesy unto you a false vision and divination, and a thing of nought, and the deceit of their heart"**, meaning, the preachers are telling the people stuff that supposedly God said, but in actuality God did not say such a thing, which makes the preaching false, and therefore not benefiting anybody (in vain), except maybe the preacher, you know, in making him look extra holy, for his own benefit, which a lot of preachers tend to do, especially prosperity gospel preachers, you know what I mean!?

Ok, let's check out the second scripture that stood out to me pertaining to this commandment, and it's; Leviticus 19:12 (KJV), and it says, **"And ye shall not swear by my name falsely, neither shalt thou profane the name of thy God: I *am* the LORD"**. So, this scripture is telling us not to use God's name in a lie and not to disrespect His name, as in blasphemy, because God's name is Holy, and we need to treat it as such, otherwise we will be using it "in vain." Ok, that's all I got for this commandment, I encourage you to double check this commandment for yourself, pray on it, and see what understanding you come out with!

4th Commandment

KJV-Exodus 20:8-11; **"Remember the sabbath day, to keep it holy. Six days shalt thou labour, and do all thy work: but the seventh day *is* the sabbath of the LORD thy God: *in it* thou shalt not do any work, thou, nor thy son, nor thy daughter, thy manservant, nor thy maidservant, nor thy cattle, nor thy stranger that *is* within thy gates: For *in* six days the LORD made heaven and earth, the sea, and all that in them *is*, and rested the seventh day: wherefore the LORD blessed the sabbath day, and hallowed it."**

This commandment is pretty much self-explanatory, because it's pretty much just telling us that God has reserved one day out of the week for us to keep holy, you know, a day that we can put a pause on our busy lives and take our time to remember and honor God, our creator. Now, which day is the Sabbath really on, is it Saturday or Sunday? And the reason why I ask this is because, the commandment says that the seventh's day of the week is the Sabbath day, but most Christians (including myself) observe the Sabbath on Sundays, why is that, shouldn't we be observing it on Saturdays, which is the actual seventh day of the week!? I've actually been wondering about this question for a while now, but I've never really searched out the scriptures and or do any research to find out why it was changed from Saturday to Sunday, so I'm guessing this would be a good time for me to finally search it out and see whether we are observing the Sabbath on the wrong day (Sundays) or not. So give me some time, hang on tight, and I'll be right back with my answer on this question soon!

Hey, ok, I'm back, I'm done researching whether the Sabbath should be on Saturday or Sunday! It took me about a day and a half of intense searching, first searching through the Bible to see what more it had to say about the Sabbath, and whether or not the Bible changed it from Saturday to Sunday after Christ died (as I thought that might be the reason for the change), and then I searched the internet to see what others had to say about the Sabbath and get some historical facts and stuff like that. And so, well, I've got the answer, and I'm sorry to say, but from everything I checked out, the Sabbath day is actually Saturday, not Sunday. And the reason why I've concluded that Saturday is actually the Sabbath day is because, nowhere in the Bible does it say that the Sabbath was changed to the first day of the week (which is Sunday) instead of the seventh day of the week (which is Saturday), which is the day that God had blessed and made it a holy day. And then, after I finished searching out the Bible, I went to the internet to see why, when and how was the Sabbath day changed from Saturday to Sunday, you know, I went to the internet to see if there was a legitimate reason for the change. But, the reasons I found were far from legit, they were actually more disturbing than not. And the reason why I say disturbing is because, I found out that, the Sunday Sabbath observance actually came from the pagan tradition, you know the pagans used to worship their sun god on Sundays, thereby, when the emperor of Rome (Constantine) converted to Christianity, he got the Sabbath switched from Saturday to Sunday. And the reason why he switched it is because Sunday is the day of the week he and his people were used to worshiping their sun god, and so he switched it so as to make it easier for him to get his people to convert to Christianity by not losing the day they were used to worshiping their sun god Mithras (and you can easily do this research for yourself, just go to the internet and type in "How the Sabbath was changed", and you'll be amazed at what you read.

Man, is that crazy or not, we have actually gotten our Sunday Sabbath worshipping from the pagans, I mean we have actually abandon keeping the Sabbath (Saturday) holy as God commanded us to do, but instead we went along with the pagan Sunday worshipping, and we've done this for more than a thousand and more years. Man, how did that happen, how and or why did the Christians at the time just accept this change, and why hasn't it been corrected all this time? Ok, so let's go back and just check it out real quick how it happened. And what happened was, the emperor of Rome at the time (Constantine), was getting ready to go to war, then one day he looked up at the sky and saw something that he construed as being of a divine nature, which he interpreted as being a sign that he should convert to Christianity and by doing so God would be on his side and give him victory over his enemy (this was around the fourth century). And so after he converted into Christianity, he made Christianity the religion of the Roman empire and also started installing a lot of his people into high ranks in the churches, which made it easier for the sun worshipping Romans to mix and or influence their pagan traditions (like Christmas and Easter, which we'll talk about more later in the book, in their own chapter) into Christianity. And one of those traditions was worshipping their sun god on the first day of the week (which is Sunday). So not long after he converted to Christianity, and as a way to not anger his people by making them worship God on Saturday instead of Sunday (as they were used to doing for their sun god), Constantine decided to declare Sunday as the official day of rest and worship for all Christians.

And so, I'm sure a lot of the Christians at the time must have rebelled the order, but it looks like overtime they just got worn out and gave in, and therefor Sunday worshipping ended up becoming the norm, replacing Saturday as the holy day. Man, is this crazy or what? I mean this is terrible, because this means most of us Christians are worshipping on the wrong day, you know, we trying to keep the Sabbath holy, but the Sabbath is actually on Saturday, not Sunday.

Man, I feel terrible right about now, I mean, this is really sad! I wish I had read the Bible sooner, because all these years that I tried to keep

Sunday holy, only to find out now (when I'm 42 years old) that I have been keeping the wrong day holy is really starting to make me feel kinda sad. And I'm not sad that I kept Sunday holy (because I just didn't know any better, that is what I was taught), I'm sad that it took me this long to really start reading the Bible and search out the truth. And actually, sad is not the right word, the right word is disappointed. And the reason why I'm disappointed in myself is because, I had a feeling that the Sabbath might actually be on Saturdays, but I just went along with Sunday because I just figured there must be a good reason why it was changed to Sunday, you know, I was just too lazy to search out the truth, you know, just like a lot of other Christians.

Oh man, this is heavy, I'm really having a hard time gathering my thoughts right now, and I can feel my chest starting to get kinda tight, and my breathing is starting to get heavy, oh man, oh man is all I can really think right now, oh man, Lord help us, we Christians are lost! And this is the reason why I decided to call this book "Christianity Lost", and it's because the more I read the Bible, the more discrepancies I keep finding that don't align with the way we are practicing our Christianity and what the Bible says. I mean, it's almost like we just going through the motions and no one is doing some fact checking so as to set us straight, you know what I mean? Or, maybe there are people out there who do know the truth, and who are trying to tell it to us, but maybe we are just so set in our ways that we refuse to hear them, because we don't want to know and or accept the truth. And the reason why we tend to refuse to accept the truth is because we tend to have become so comfortable in our own practice of Christianity that we become unwilling to change, even if that change is what is needed in order to be in obedience to the Bible. And this is why a huge mistake like this (observing the Sabbath on the wrong day) can continue year after year, decade after decade, century after century, and it's because people just get used to it, you know, people just accept it (Sunday Sabbath) and just roll with it.

It's amazing to me that we Christians are ok with disobeying God by observing the Sabbath on the wrong day. I mean, it's very puzzling to me that there's no real movement within the Christian community that is talking about this, or, maybe there is, but maybe their voices are just not loud enough. And actually, there are a few churches that do observe their Sabbaths on Saturdays (with the Seventh-day Adventist being the largest of them) but their voices are not loud enough to get most other Churches and or Christians to pay attention to them. And the interesting thing is, I've always known about the Seventh-day Adventists Churches, but I don't know much about their doctrine except that they go to church on Saturdays instead of Sundays, you know, unlike most Christians, which always puzzled me. But now I know why they maintain their Sabbath day on Saturdays, and it's because they read the Bible and realized that the Bible never changed the Sabbath to Sunday, therefor they kept Saturday as their Sabbath day, which is what the rest of us Christians need to do.

Man, we are really lost, just going through the motion, sleep walking through our Christianity, almost like the blind leading the blind, you know, I can't believe it, I really just can't believe it! I can't believe that with all these preachers, pastors, ministers, priests, and even the Pope and etc., you know, people that are supposed to be very well versed in the Bible, people that are supposed to be the shepherds, you know, people that are supposed to be the leaders of the churches and or denominations, I can't believe that they all are willing to just go ahead and observe the Sabbath on the wrong day. I mean, how can all these people misinterpret the Bible, you know, I mean, I just don't believe that they don't know that they are observing the Sabbath on the wrong day, you know, because these people are supposed to be pretty much Bible scholars, you know what I mean!? And so I truly refuse to believe that most of them don't know that the Sabbath is actually on Saturday instead of Sunday, but for whatever reason (I'm sure Satan has something to do with this) they are choosing not to raise the topic (so a correction can be made), in which case they are really doing a spiritual injustice to their congregations, you know, because they are supposed to be the shepherds, thereby, they are supposed to feed their congregations the truth, and not doing so is just as bad as feeding their congregations lies. KJV-Ezekiel 22:26; **"Her priests have violated my law, and have profaned mine holy things: they have put no difference between the holy and profane, neither have they shewed *difference* between the** unclean and the clean, and have hid their eyes from my sabbaths, and I am profaned among them."

So, my fellow Christians, this is bad news, because we have actually been disobeying Gods' Sabbath commandment, we have not been keeping the Sabbath (Saturday) holy. So I don't know about you, but I no longer gonna do my Sabbath observance on Sundays, from now on I'm gonna be keeping my Sabbath holy on Saturdays (to the best of my abilities). It's gonna be a challenge to change observing the Sabbath on Saturdays instead of Sundays, and it's because the world is pretty much set for Sunday to be the day of rest (as most peoples' days off from work and other activities is Sundays), and since Sunday has been ingrained in my brain as the "holy day" of the week since I was little, it's gonna be hard to switch my brain to Saturday, but, the truth is the truth, and since I wanna be in obedience to the word of God, I must adhere to the truth, and that's what this book is all about, it's for me to uncover the real truth of the Bible, and of course for me to share whatever truths I find with as many other people as I can, you know, so we can all be on the right path to better ourselves as Christians, and worship God in truth and with a pure heart, you know, because otherwise all our prayers, worship and etc., will pretty much just be "in vain". So I encourage you to go and check out the Bible and compare scripture with scripture and ask God to reveal the true meaning of the verses, that way you can know the truth for yourself, and of course, always share the truth with others, so they too can worship God in truth!

5th Commandment

KJV-Exodus 20:12; "**Honour thy father and thy mother: that thy days may be long upon the land which the LORD thy God giveth thee**".

So, this commandment wants us to honor our parents, but, what does it really mean to honor our parents!? I believe honoring our parents really means not only to respect them, but it also means to not bring shame to their names, you know, not to do stupid stuff that will bring shame to them, but to do good in our lives, so as to make them be proud to be our parents, you know what I mean? Also, honoring our parents also means taking care of them when they become older (old age), you know, so they can live out the rest of their golden years with dignity and respect that they deserve, you know, for all the hard work and sacrifice they put in to raise you right. And so, this is the reason why God wants us to honor our parents, and it's because; these are the people God chose for us to be born through, you know, these are the people that God chose to be our guardians and raise us until we are old enough to take care of ourselves, and therefore God holds them to a high regard, and so He wants us to hold our parents in high regard as well, you know, by honoring them!

6th Commandment

KJV-Exodus 20:13; **"Thou shalt not kill"**.

This Commandment is self-explanatory, it's telling us that we should not take other people's lives, you know, it's telling us not to commit murder. And the reason why God gave us this commandment is to make sure that we understand that every life matters, you know every person is valuable in God's eyes, and therefor nobody has the right to destroy His most valuable creation, which is us, human beings.

Now, what about soldiers, or police, or other people whose jobs might require them to kill, does this commandment forbid them from killing as well, even though their jobs might require it? I'm not a hundred percent sure of my answer to this question, but I believe that if your job might require you to kill if need be, I don't think God will hold that against you. And the reason why I say this is because, I believe that if you are a soldier (for example) and get sent out to war and you end up having to kill people (the enemy), that killing will be in defense of your nation, therefor that killing will be in behalf of your country, you know, it will be in defense of your country against an enemy that wants to destroy it and its people, you know what I mean!?

It's kinda tricky, but armies and police are necessary in the world, because there's always gonna be bad groups of people in the world that look to cause mayhem and or victimize innocent people and or countries, therefor armies and police are needed to provide law and order in the world, otherwise there would be anarchy and or chaos in the world. Now, of course if a soldier, or a police officer, or any other person in authority abuse their powers and end up killing innocent people unjustifiably, then that there is murder, and that person will be guilty of violating this commandment.

And so, this commandment is pretty much talking about murder, you know, not killing people just because, you know, not killing people just because you mad at them, or because you hate them, or because you jealous of them, or because you wanna steal from them, and or other reasons like that, you know what I mean? It's crazy, but there are a lot of people out there killing other people for no damn good reason, you know, they killing other people for small silly stuff, stupid stuff! And this is why God gave us this commandment, and that is so we know that God will hold us accountable for any killing we do, because every life is precious, and so we are not to kill it, for no just cause!

7th **Commandment**

KJV-Exodus 20:14; **"Thou shalt not commit adultery"**.

Adultery, adultery, adultery, sex outside the marriage, this commandment has got to be one of the hardest for most people to keep, you know what I mean!? And the reason I say this is because, it seems like most marriages usually end because of adultery, you know, because someone in the marriage cheated (usually the guy, right, lol). I don't know what it is, but sex is a very powerful urge, you know, the desire for it is very strong (especially the desire for new sex), so strong that a lot of people are unable to control it, and this is why a lot of people end up having sex outside of their marriages, and it's because they fall victim to their urges. Now, did you notice how I said "they fall victim to their urges!?" And the reason why I said that is because I truly believe that no one gets married with the thought that they will continue to have sex with other people, you know, most people get married because they truly love the person they are marrying and accept the fact that they are vowing not to have sex with anybody else except their wife or husband. And so, this is why I call people who end up in extra marital affairs "victims of their urges", and it's because they usually find themselves in these situations because they just could not control and or could not tame their sexual urges (for others), for whatever reason. And what I mean by control and or tame is that, most people who have affairs outside their marriage, it's usually because something in their marriage is not working right, you know, the couple is having some issues in their marriage that is affecting their desire for intimacy with each other, and so therefor, if this lack of intimacy keeps going for a long period of time, sooner or later one of them will start looking outside the marriage for some intimacy and or just some sexual healing, you know what I mean?

    Man, it's crazy, but that sex thing is a very powerful urge, and if it's not controlled and or tamed, it is very easy for most people (especially man) to find themselves in some extra marital situations. And did you notice how I parenthesized "especially man" in the sentence above? And the reason why I said especially man, it's because man tend to be the ones that easily get caught up in extra marital situations than women. And the reason for this is because men tend to be a lot weaker in controlling their sex urges than women, you know, women are better at controlling their lust than men are. And the reason why men are weaker in controlling their lust is because, men are made to be hunters, you know, the same way men are made to instantly be hunters for food, is the same way men are made to be hunters for sex, you know what I mean, lol? And what I mean is, us men, God gave us so much testosterone that if we go a few weeks without sex, our minds and our bodies start to shiver, you know, our minds start not to be able to concentrate right, and our bodies literally start to shake, lol, you know what I mean fellows, lol!?

    And this is why a lot of guys who are not married tend to cheat on their girlfriends a lot more than not, and it's because they don't necessary feel the need to control and or tame their sexual urges, you know, because after all, they are not married, which means they have not taken the vow of being with just one women, and therefore, if their girlfriends are not measuring up to their sexual needs, they easily just go find another girl who is ready, willing and able to give them some sexual healing. And this is why a lot of girls find themselves getting cheated on by their boyfriends, and it doesn't mean that the boy doesn't like them anymore, it just means that the boy chose not to tame their sexual urge, which is easier to do when he is not married. And so, likewise, guys who are married, they too can find themselves in a relationship that is not measuring up to their sexual needs, and therefore they too can find themselves looking for another women that is willing, ready and able to provide that sexual healing. And also, just like how when a boy cheats on his girlfriend it usually doesn't mean that he doesn't like her anymore, well it's the same thing as when a married men cheats on his wife, it doesn't mean that he doesn't love her anymore, it just means that he was (for whatever reason) unable to control his sexual urges. And this is why God gave us this commandment, and it's because, only under marriage are people more likely than not will do a much better job of controlling their sexual urges, you know, only under marriage are people more willing to tame their sexual urges and make sure that they don't cheat on their spouses. And the reason why I say this is because, under marriage, people take their relationships much more seriously, and not only that, but they know that if they cheat, they are not only cheated on their spouses, but they know that they will be breaking this commandment, especially if they are Christians who want to be right with the Lord. And so, this is why God gave us this commandment, so we can work harder in taming our sexual desires for others, that way we can maintain our marriages, which are sacred in God's eyes.

And so, marriages can be hard to maintain sometimes, and this is because, when people get marriage, that means they are merging their lives together in a much more serious way, meaning, instead of thinking of themselves in singular (as when they were single), now they have to think of themselves in plural, you know, whatever decisions they make, they have to make them with the other person in mind. And so, it can be hard sometimes to merge two unique personalities into oneness, you know, merging two individuals to be able to function as one unit. And this is why a lot of marriages fail, and it's because a lot of people don't master the art of being married, which is, knowing how the other person functions, therefore each partner will know how to maneuver within the relationship so as to work as a functioning unit, you know, it's like knowing each other's strengths and weaknesses so well that it makes it easier for y'all to pick up the slack and or know how to up lift each other as needed, because that is what marriage is all about, you know, looking out for each other, so as to make sure that the both of you are in good shape (in mind, body and spirit), so that instead of having to deal with a bunch of conflict in your marriage, the two of you can actually have a good working and loving relationship, so that intimacy can be a regular part of enjoying each other, as what marriage was intended for, you know, to be fruitful and multiply, or as the Bible says; **"Marriage [is] honourable in all, and the bed undefiled"** (KJV-Hebrews 13:4).

8th Commandment

KJV-Exodus 20:15; **"Thou shalt not steal"**.

It's amazing how many people out there have no problem stealing, you know, it's amazing how people can consciously involve themselves in a lifestyle of thievery without even feeling guilty about it, you know what I mean!? It's crazy, but there are a lot of people out there that actually make a living from stealing, you know, either from being small time crooks (petty thieves) and or big time crooks (robbers/buglers). I mean it's crazy, but there are people out there that actually make stealing a profession (white color crimes, blue color crimes, internet scams, and so on). Now, I know that life can be very tough sometimes, I know that people can get very desperate to the point where they see stealing as the only option they have for them to survive, but, taking other people's things is still wrong, it's still stealing, and it's still immoral. And this is why God gave us this commandment, and it's to let us know that we should not take things that belong to other people without their permission. And I mean, I know that people can get very desperate (and this is when stealing usually happens, but stealing is stealing, whether it's small time or large scale, it's still stealing, and God definitely forbids it!

9th Commandment

> KJV-Exodus 20:16; **"Thou shalt not bear false witness against thy neighbour".**

This commandment is pretty clear and direct, because what it's saying is, don't lie on people, you know, stop telling lies about people, if you don't know about a person, stop making up stuff about people, you know, stop wrongly accusing people of stuff that you have no evidence to prove they did something, you know what I mean!? And so, all y'all people that like to gossip about people (without any proof), stop it, because otherwise you will be bearing a false witness against your neighbor. And neighbor don't just mean your actual next door neighbor, nope, neighbor in the Bible means anybody in the world, whether they are near or far, in the Bible they are still considered your neighbor. So this commandment is telling us not to lie on people, because lies can end up bringing harm to people's character and or physically, for no fault of their own, and this is why God forbids it!

10th Commandment

> KJV-Exodus 20:17; **"Thou shalt not covet thy neighbour's house, thou shalt not covet thy neighbour's wife, nor his manservant, nor his maidservant, nor his ox, nor his ass, nor any thing that *is* thy neighbour's".**

This commandment is very interesting, because all I can think of is, what were they doing back in the Bible days to cause God to give this commandment, you know what I mean? I mean, I'm thinking something crazy must have been going on back then to where God had to say, hey, look, stop desiring other people's houses and wives and servants and animals and other stuff, you know, God had to put a stop to people trying to take other people's houses and wives and so on. I mean, that's crazy right, if that is what was going on back then, that's pretty wild, right? I mean, I can just imagine someone saying to themselves, man, he sure got a nice house, and he sure got a beautiful wife, and he sure got some good servants, and he sure got some healthy looking animals, and what about all that nice stuff he got in the house, oh man, you know what, I got have that, I gotta take those from him! I mean, it's crazy, but there is a possibility that could have been going on, you know what I mean?

And then, maybe God was just giving them this commandment as a precautionary action, you know, so they won't even think about desiring other people's houses, or other people's wives, and so on and so on. It's like, God was telling them (as He's telling us now), don't even think about it, you know, stop desiring other people's stuff and go get your own stuff, you know what I mean? And so yeah, that is exactly what this commandment is about, it's a precaution, you know, God knows that if we desire something so much, He knows we might eventually act on it and try to take it for our self, you know, we might even cause harm to our neighbor so we can have their stuff. I mean it's like, if someone has a beautiful wife, and if you desire her so much, you might bring harm to the husband just so you can have his wife. I mean, I'm sure you have heard the stories where people kill other people's significant other's so that they can be with the person they desire. I mean, there are movies that have been made about stories like this, you know, where someone is so obsessed with another person's significant other that they are willing to kill, just so they can be with that person. And so, this is why God gave us this commandment, you know, to tell us that we shouldn't even be thinking about taking other people's houses, wives, husbands, and or etc!

3

FORNICATION

I used to wonder why God never made fornication part of the Ten Commandments, I mean, with fornication being probably the sin that most people commit, doesn't it seem like it should be part of the Ten Commandments, and or maybe there should have been 11 commandments, you know, with fornication as one of the commandments!? And the reason why I say this is because, God gave us the Ten Commandments so as to emphasize the behaviors that He deems very immoral, you know, therefor we are not to engage in them. And so, I'm thinking, if sex before marriage was just as immoral as the Ten Commandments, I'm thinking, shouldn't it also be part of the Ten Commandments? And then so I started thinking, maybe sex before marriage is not a immoral as the acts in the Ten Commandments, you know, because if they were, I'm pretty sure God would have included them in the Ten Commandments, you know what I mean? But then, I started thinking, to God a sin is a sin, you know, to God there's no such thing as a smaller sin or a bigger sin, you know, to God a sin is a sin, all deserving the same punishment (hell)!

And then so, I started thinking again, well, maybe sex before marriage is actually not a sin after all. And the reason why I say this is because, not only is fornication not part of the Ten Commandments, but I was really having a hard time thinking why would God want to punish us for having sex, you know, when He put so much sexual urges in us and told us to go be fruitful and multiply. And also, I was thinking, why would God want to punish us when He already knew that most likely than not we would not be able to wait until we are married to start having sex, you know, unless we all start getting married from when we are teenagers, you know, the age which our sex drives usually starts to peak out of control, you know what I mean, lol!?

And so yeah, I was really having a hard time believing that sex before marriage was actually sin, because if it was, then most people (who are not married) would have a hard time trying not to commit this sin. And the reason why I say this is because, we are pretty much sexual beings, I mean, we were made to be sexually active, and so it is very hard for most of us to tame our sexual urges, and therefore, waiting until we are married to have sex is almost impossible, you know, unless we are very, very, very discipline, which most of us are not. And did you notice how I said "unless we are very, very, very discipline?" And the reason why I said that is because, it is very hard for most of us to fight our nature, and so for us to be able to tame our nature we pretty much gonna have to go against our nature, which means we will have to be discipline enough to handle and or control our sexual urges, which can be very challenging, especially nowadays. And the reason why I say "especially nowadays" is because, it seems like nowadays almost everything around us, and or, it seems like almost everywhere we turn we are bombarded with either images and or messages about sex. I mean, it's almost like we can't escape not seeing and or hearing about sex every day, in one form or another, you know, whether it's from music, movies, T.V. shows, magazines, the internet, and so on. And so, this is also why sexual activities seem to be on the rise every year among young people, and it's because they are exposed to sexual images and messages so much that makes it very hard for them to be able to tame their sexual urges. And I mean, if we adults seem to be having a hard time taming our sexual urges, how much more harder do you think it must be for teenagers to try and tame their sexual urges. I mean it's crazy, but we are sexual beings, and if we don't learn how to tame our sexual urges we can easily find ourselves engaging in sex before marriage.

Now, with all this been said, I of course had to go and search out the Bible and see what it had to say about fornication, because that is what we have to do, you know, we can't just come up with a theory and or an understanding based on what we think or feel is the correct meaning of anything that has to do with spirituality and or the Bible. And so I went and searched out the Bible, and I found out something interesting about the word "fornication". And what I found out is, the word "fornication" in the Bible actually does not mean sex before marriage, nope, the word "fornication" actually means "sexual immorality". And how I found this out is by going to the internet and searching out the word "fornication", so I can see where the word fornication comes from in its original language that it was translated from. So I found out that the word fornication comes from the Greek word "porneia", which means "sexual immorality" in the Greek language, which is the language most of the current Bibles are translated from.

And then so, I went back to the Bible and checked out all the verses that talks about fornication, and I did not find any verses that seemed to be using fornication to mean sex before marriage, most of the verses seem to use fornication to mean sexual immorality. And the interesting thing is, I did not find any verse that has the word fornication and marriage in it, but I did find a verse that did have the word fornication and divorce in it, let's check it out: KJV-Matthew 5:32; **"But I say unto you, That whosoever shall put away his wife, saving for the cause of fornication, causeth her to commit adultery: and whosoever shall marry her that is divorced committeth adultery"**. Ok, see how it says "saving for the cause of fornication", so to me, that must mean some kind of immorality, most likely adultery, because the couple has already married, so it can't be sex before marriage, otherwise it would have said something like "saving for the cause of uncleanness" or "saving for the cause of finding her not to be a virgin", you know, something like that. Let's check out some more verses with the word fornication in it: KJV-Ezekiel 16:15; **"But thou didst trust in thine own beauty, and playedst the harlot because of thy renown, and pouredst out thy fornications on every one that passed by; his it was"**. Did you see how it says **"trust in thine own beauty"**, which means, she knew she looked good, you know, had that sex appeal. Also, see how it says **"and playedst the harlot"**, which means, prostituted herself. And so, see how it says **"and pouredst out thy fornications on every one that passed by"**, which means, she seduced every one that passed by and gave them some sex. Wow, it seems like prostitution was a big thing going on even back in the Bible days, and it looks like to me this is the sexual immorality that the word fornication is mostly used for, but it's also used for other sexual immorality as well, let's check out some more verses: KJV-1 Corinthians 5:1; **"It is reported commonly that there is fornication among you, and such fornication as is not so much as named among the Gentiles, that one should have his father's wife."** Oooh, did you catch the sexual immorality in this verse, **"that one should have his father's wife"**, oh man, looks like someone slept with their own father's wife, how wicked is that, and why did she go along with it, or did she seduce him, wait a minute, was this his own mother or a step mother, oh well, it don't matter, wicked all the same, shame, shame, shame, shame, lol. But did you see there, another form of fornication, dude slept with his own father's wife, crazy right, it seems like people were really wilding out back in the Bible days, come to think of it, people are still wilding out even nowadays, you know what I mean, smh!?

Anyway, let's check out some more verses with the word fornication in it: KJV-Jude 1:7; **"Even as Sodom and Gomorrha, and the cities about them in like manner, giving themselves over to fornication, and going after strange flesh, are set forth for an example, suffering the vengeance of eternal fire"**. Ok, remember the story of Sodom and Gomorrha, you know, where God ended up destroying the whole city because of all the sexual wickedness that was going on, well, that's what this verse is talking about. And you see how it says, **"giving themselves over to fornication, and going after strange flesh"**, well the sexual immorality in this verse is homosexuality (strange flesh). Let's check out some more verses: KJV-Ezekiel 16:26; **"Thou hast also committed fornication with the Egyptians thy neighbours, great of flesh; and hast increased thy whoredoms, to provoke me to anger."** The sexual immorality in this verse is promiscuousness (whoredoms), you know, sleeping with a whole bunch of people, you know what I mean? Ok, let's just check out one more verse and we should be done on this part, you know, me trying to make my point on what the word fornication really means, lol. Let's check out: KJVJ-1 Corinthians 6:18; "**Flee fornication. Every sin that a man doeth is without the body; but he that committeth fornication sinneth against his own body**". Ok, so this verse is telling us that we should stay away from sexual immorality, and it also says that when we engage in sexual immorality we actually sinning against our own bodies, you know, unlike other sins, the sin of fornication is actually against our own bodies, meaning, we are using our bodies immorally (sexually), you know what I mean?

Now, since I have successfully proven that fornication really means sexual immorality than sex before marriage (lol), the question is, is sex before marriage still a sin or not!? I will attempt to answer this question the best I can, using the scriptures of course. And the reason why I say I will attempt the best I can, it's because there's no scripture that actually comes out right and says anything about sex before marriage, but there are a few scriptures that do suggest sex before marriage may be a sin and or may just be strongly looked down upon. Anyway, let's check out some scriptures and see what they say!

KJV-Exodus 22:16-17; "**And if a man entice a maid that is not betrothed, and lie with her, he shall surely endow her to be his wife. If her father utterly refuse to give her unto him, he shall pay money according to the dowry of virgins**". Oh oh, did you hear what this verse just said, it said, if a man seduces a woman and has sex with her, he should seek to make her his wife, but, if her father refuses to give him the woman so she can be his wife, then he has to pay the father some money equivalent to the dowry of virgins! Ok, so, this is a very interesting verse, and the reason why I say this is because, it looks like here we have a man and a woman having sex before marriage, and the interesting thing is, instead of them being punished and or ostracized for their sex before marriage activity, it looks like if the guy makes an attempt to marry her but her father refuses (nowadays it would be the woman herself making the decision whether to marry him or not, in most countries anyway), the guy can just pay for taking her virginity (nowadays virginity is not as highly regarded as it used to be) and keep on stepping, lol, you know what I mean!? So, this verse definitely doesn't seem to suggest that sex before marriage is a sin, it just says that the guy should try to marry the woman that he has sex with. Ok, let's check out some more verses!

KJV-Hebrews 13:4; **"Marriage *is* honourable in all, and the bed undefiled: but whoremongers and adulterers God will judge"**. Ok, so, this verse talks about marriage being good and the bed untainted, and also it talks about God judging adulterers (those who have sex outside their marriages) and whoremongers (those who are promiscuous and or those who have sex with prostitutes). So, nothing about sex before marriage in this verse, so let's continue, let's check out some more verses!

KJV- Deuteronomy 22:13-21&28-29; **"If any man take a wife, and go in unto her, and hate her,**

14 And give occasions of speech against her, and bring up an evil name upon her, and say, I took this woman, and when I came to her, I found her not a maid:

15 Then shall the father of the damsel, and her mother, take and bring forth *the tokens of* the damsel's virginity unto the elders of the city in the gate:

16 And the damsel's father shall say unto the elders, I gave my daughter unto this man to wife, and he hateth her;

17 And, lo, he hath given occasions of speech *against her*, saying, I found not thy daughter a maid; and yet these *are the tokens of* my daughter's virginity. And they shall spread the cloth before the elders of the city.

18 And the elders of that city shall take that man and chastise him;

19 And they shall amerce him in an hundred *shekels* of silver, and give *them* unto the father of the damsel, because he hath brought up an evil name upon a virgin of Israel: and she shall be his wife; he may not put her away all his days.

20 But if this thing be true, *and the tokens of* virginity be not found for the damsel:

21 Then they shall bring out the damsel to the door of her father's house, and the men of her city shall stone her with stones that she die: because she hath wrought folly in Israel, to play the whore in her father's house: so shalt thou put evil away from among you.

28 If a man find a damsel *that is* a virgin, which is not betrothed, and lay hold on her, and lie with her, and they be found;

29 Then the man that lay with her shall give unto the damsel's father fifty *shekels* of silver, and she shall be his wife; because he hath humbled her, he may not put her away all his days". Ok, wow, these are some interesting verses, aren't they!? I mean, they talking about stoning the women to death if she's found not to be a virgin when she gets married. My only question is, what about the man, was the man required to be a virgin also before he got married, or was it just the woman who was required to be a virgin before marriage? And the reason why I ask this is because the Bible seems to have a lot to say about woman being virgins before married but almost nothing about guys having to be virgins, you know what I mean? I mean, the most the Bible says about guys is that they should try to be virgins, but if they can't then it's best if they get married. And so to me, it looks like virginity was highly regarded for women, and as for men, they were required to marry any woman that they happen to have sex with who was a virgin, but as far as women who were not virgins, not much is said about them. And actually, I think that any woman that was not a virgin was considered to be a whole, and I don't think it mattered whether the woman had sex with a bunch of guys or just one person, you know, like if she had a boyfriend and just had sex with just the boyfriend, you know, I think back in the Bible days she would still be considered a whore, you know what I mean!?

Man, wow, these verses can be kinda tricky discern sometimes, and I think is why a lot of people have a hard time interpreting them, you know, and end up coming up with understandings that are way off what the Bible actually meant to say. And I think this is why most people thought and or still think that fornication actually means "sex before marriage", and it's because virginity was so regarded back in the Bible days that most people just figured that fornication must have meant sex before marriage, but in actuality, fornication actually means "sexual immorality". And sexual immorality is engaging in sexual activities that render us unclean and or wicked, you know, like; incest, prostitution, promiscuousness, adultery, homosexuality, beastiality, swinging, open marriages, and so on. Now, with all this being said, I'm not ready to declare that sex before marriage is not a sin, but I have a feeling that the reason why men were encouraged to marry any virgin they had sex with is because if they didn't, then this would have meant that there would have been a lot of women that would not have been suitable for marriage, you know, because their virginity (which represented their worth and or their virtuousness) would have already been taken away by another man, which would have rendered the woman worthless and or unclean, and no man would want to marry them, you know, because back then it looks like the men only wanted to marry virgins, you know, they wanted to know that their wives were pure, you know, untouched by any other man before them, you know what I mean!? And it's interesting how virginity is not as must of a big deal nowadays, I mean, nowadays it don't seem like men really care much whether their wives are virgins or not before they marry them, you know? I mean, nowadays it seems like guys just hope that their wives did not have a bunch of boyfriends before they marry them, you know what I mean guys, lol.

And so yeah, back in the Bible days virginity was a big deal, and men did not want to marry a woman who was not a virgin, but nowadays, men don't really worry too much about whether or not their wives are virgins or not, oh no, nowadays what guys most worry about is whether their wives already have a bunch of kids or not, you know what I mean, lol. I mean, am I right or wrong, hey fellows, am I right or wrong!? And this is why a lot of women who tend to have a lot of kids before they are married tend to have a hard time finding a husband, you know, and it's because most guys just don't really want to marry a women who has already given another guy a bunch of kids, you know, because in this instance, the guy sees the woman as not being as pure, you know, the other man's kids kind of serve as a reminder to the guy that the woman he is dating has already been touched by another man, and not just touched once, but touched a whole bunch of times, you know what I mean? And this is also why a lot of women who have kids by a bunch of men tend to have even a harder time not only finding a husband, but harder time even finding and or keeping a boyfriend, and it's because the guys she dates kinda see her as just good enough to date, but not good enough to make them their girlfriends, let alone to make them their wife. And so this is why women should try their best not to have kids before they are married, because it's very easy for a woman to find herself with two or more baba daddies if they are not careful, you know what I mean? And truth be told, most guys are not really ready to be fathers unless they are married (to the mother of their children), and this is why there are so many absent fathers out there, and it's because since the fathers are not married to their kids mother, it is very easy for them to take the easy way out and just remove themselves from their parental responsibilities. And so (ladies), please try your best not to have kids with guys before they marry you (which can easily be done nowadays, especially with all these birth control stuff they got out there, all you gotta do is go to your doctor and tell them that you need a birth control that will make sure you don't get pregnant until you are married and I'm sure they give you some advice on witch ones to use, lol, I'm serious, don't mind my laughter, you know, they got stuff that can make sure you won't get pregnant for five or ten years, you know, just in case you are having a hard time holding on to your virginity, lol), otherwise you can easily find yourself raising those kids by yourself, and not only that, but it will make it even harder to get another guy to marry you, you know, because guys nowadays are already scared of marriage, and so the thought of marrying a woman who already has kids by someone else can scare them even more about marrying that woman, you know what I mean ladies!?

And so anyway, back to our sex before marriage topic, I just wanna say, don't just take my word for it, I strongly encourage you to read and search out the Bible for yourself, and, if you find a verse that you believe can correct my thinking on this sex before marriage matter, I strongly urge you to send me an email so I can double check on it, because this is what we Christians are supposed to do, you know, double check the scriptures so we can make corrections to our understanding of it, and so I'm open to being corrected on any topic that I discuss in this book. Ok, I got one more verse that I want us to check out before we conclude this chapter! KJV- 1 Thessalonians 4:3-5; **"For this is the will of God, *even* your sanctification, that ye should abstain from fornication: That every one of you should know how to possess his vessel in sanctification and honour; Not in the lust of concupiscence, even as the Gentiles which know not God:"** Ok so, this verse is telling us that we should all (as Christians) know how to keep our bodies in sanctification and honor, you know, and not lust after sexual immorality like other people in the world, who don't know God!

And so, yeah, fornication does not mean sex before marriage, it means all manners of sexual immorality, but, if you wanna include sex before marriage as another form of sexual immorality, please feel free to do so, trust me, I won't argue with you on it, because one thing that I do know, I know that God wants us to be holy in both mind, body and spirit, and so if sex before marriage makes us unholy, then it's something that we should definitely try our best to avoid. Ok, I hope I didn't confuse anybody in this fornication chapter, but I'm here to search out the Bible for truth, and sometimes that truth can be hard to explain, and this is why we all need each other as Christians, you know, so we can work and or help each other in our spiritual journeys as we aim to be better Christians!

4

DOCTRINE

I used to wonder why there were so many church denominations, but as I got older I started to realize it's because, when people come to a truth about something in the Bible that does not support what their churches are teaching, most often than not when they bring up the subject with their church leaders, most often than not they will get a cold shoulder and or the church leaders will refuse to change the church's errors, which will leave the person no choice but to leave the church and most likely start their own church. And this is how we end up with so many denominations, and it's because a lot of churches just refuse to change part of their doctrines that might not align with what the Bible teaches, and so, most people who come to truth usually end up finding themselves unable to go along with what their churches are teaching, and therefor end up feeling like an outsider from even a church that they might have been a member since childhood, and sooner or later they will have no choice but to leave and either go find another church, or start their own church, especially if they were actually in a leadership position at their church. I mean, I don't know what it is, but churches for some reason find it very hard to correct their doctrine, you know, most churches just seem to refuse to change their doctrine, even if that doctrine is proven to be Biblically incorrect.

And this is why it is very important for people to examine their churches doctrine to make sure that it aligns with what the Bible teaches, because otherwise you can easily find yourself in a church that teaches false doctrine, which will do you no good for your spiritual growth. And this is one of the reasons why a lot of Christians just don't seem to improve their spiritual growth from year to year, you know, and it's because they are caught up in churches that don't feed them Biblical truths, and therefore, no real spiritual growth is actually fostered into the congregations. And this is one of the reasons that, even though there are billions of Christians in the world today, this is why the world keeps getting worth and worth, you know, and it's because there's not a lot of spiritual growth going on in the churches. And what I mean by spiritual growth is, I'm talking about the maturity of understanding what the Bible is actually trying to teach us about what being a Christian is all about. I mean, I truly believe that most Christians actually have no idea what being a Christian is all about, I mean, I truly believe that most Christians are just going through the motion of what their churches teaches them without examining if what they are being talk is truth or not. And this is what I mean by spiritual growth, and it's growing the understanding of what the Bible is teaching us and working to implement that understanding into our lives. And so, the reason why I say there's not much spiritual growth going on in the churches, it's because most people seem to remain as clueless about the Bible from when they were younger to when they are adults, you know, they seem to do the same things when they become adults as they used to do when they were younger. Ok, I don't think I'm doing a good job of explaining myself right here, but, let me give some examples, maybe that will help. And so, what I mean is, it's like, for example; most Christians, if they were liars when they were younger, they continue to be liars when they get older, or, if they were fornicators when they were younger, they continue to be fornicators when they get older, or, if they were selfish when they were younger, they continue to be selfish when they get older, or, if they never fed the hungry when they were younger, they continue not to feed the hungry when they get older, or, if they never visited the sick when they were younger, they continue not to visit the sick when they get older, or, if they used to observe the Sabbath on Sundays (instead of Saturday) when they were younger, they continue to observe the Sabbath on Sundays when they get older, and so on and so on, as the Bible teaches. And this is what being a Christian is all about, you know, learning the truth about what the Bible teaches and work to apply these lessons into our practice of Christianity. And this is why the Bible says: KJV-1 Corinthians 13:11; **"When I was a child, I spake as a child, I understood as a child, I thought as a child: but when I became a man, I put away childish things"**.

Ok, you see, we are supposed to have spiritual growth as Christians, you know, our understanding of the Bible and our practice of Christianity is supposed to improve as we get older. But what I have observed is, most people get some spiritual growth from when they were kids to when they become young adults, then after that most people hit stagnation, you know, most people experience no spiritual growth from their young adulthood age to their full adulthood age (unless they experience some kind of spiritual awakening). And this is the reason why most people who used to go to church when they were younger tend to fall out of church when they get older, and it's because, when they get older, the real world starts to hit them, and once the real world starts to hit them, it becomes harder for them to concentrate on their spirituality. And then so, usually they decide that they have already learned everything they need to know about Christianity and the Bible, and therefor they figure there's no need for them to go to church anymore. And this is why it's very important for churches to teach sound doctrine, you know, otherwise we gonna end up with a whole lot more Christians (who don't go to church no more) out there who are spiritually lost, you know what I mean?

And actually, there are a lot of Christians who do go to church but they are still spiritually lost. And the reason why they are lost is because their churches don't teach and or practice sound doctrine. I mean, I don't know what it is, but almost every church has part of their doctrine that is false, you know, almost every church has part of their doctrine that is man-made, you know, part of their doctrine someone just made up. And when I say "just made up", I don't mean they came up with it out of thin air (sometimes they do, that's how you get cults and other groups like that), no, usually they find a Bible verse that seems to fit with their preconceived theological theories that they believe to be true. And so it's like, once they find a verse that seems to fit into their theories, they go ahead and make that verse the basis of their doctrine, and then they start promoting and or teaching that doctrine as truth. And this is how a lot of churches end up having part of their doctrines being false, and it's because most of the churches get so comfortable with their doctrines that they neglect to compare scripture with scripture, you know, to see if there might be another scripture and or verses that might re-explain the verse that they are basing their doctrine on. And this is why the Bible says we must compare scripture with scripture, you know, so we can make sure we are on sound Biblical grounds, and if we are not, we should make the necessary corrections as needed. Ok, so, let's check out some scriptures in the Bible and see what it has to say about sound doctrine (so you don't have to just take my word for it, I want you to read it for yourself from the Bible).

KJV-Mark 7:7-9, 13; **Howbeit in vain do they worship me, teaching *for* doctrines the commandments of men.**

8 For laying aside the commandment of God, ye hold the tradition of men, *as* the washing of pots and cups: and many other such like things ye do.

9 And he said unto them, Full well ye reject the commandment of God, that ye may keep your own tradition.

13 Making the word of God of none effect through your tradition, which ye have delivered: and many such like things do ye. Ok, did you see how it said "teaching for doctrines the commandments of men", and that's that man-made doctrine that I was talking about. And did you see how it said "For laying aside the commandment of God, ye hold the tradition of men", and what I can think about here is how we have neglected to keep the Sabbath (Saturday) holy, instead we continue to worship on Sundays (a tradition that we got from the pagans who used to worship their sun god on Sundays), which is the tradition of men. Ok, let's check out some more scriptures!

KJV-Matthew 7:15; **Beware of false prophets, which come to you in sheep's clothing, but inwardly they are ravening wolves.**

KJV- 1 John 4:1; **Beloved, believe not every spirit, but try the spirits whether they are of God: because many false prophets are gone out into the world.**

KJV- 2 Timothy 4:1-5; **I charge *thee* therefore before God, and the Lord Jesus Christ, who shall judge the quick and the dead at his appearing and his kingdom;**

2 Preach the word; be instant in season, out of season; reprove, rebuke, exhort with all longsuffering and doctrine.

3 For the time will come when they will not endure sound doctrine; but after their own lusts shall they heap to themselves teachers, having itching ears;

4 And they shall turn away *their* ears from the truth, and shall be turned unto fables.

5 But watch thou in all things, endure afflictions, do the work of an evangelist, make full proof of thy ministry.

Wow, these are some good scriptures, right!? They mostly talk about beware of false prophets, right, which means false teachers. And did you see how Matthew 7:15 said, **"which come to you in sheep's clothing, but inwardly they are ravening wolves"**, wow, strong words, right!? And then did you see how 2 Timothy 4:2 said, **"reprove, rebuke, exhort with all

longsuffering and doctrine", and this here is talking to the church leaders, and it's telling them not to quit pushing (exhort) sound doctrine, and to criticize (reprove) and disapprove (rebuke) any false doctrine. And then verses 3, 4 and 5 says (paraphrasing); it says, there will come a time that Christians will not want to hear sound doctrine, but they will look for pastors and or churches that preach what they want to hear, but these verses are telling the church leaders not to succumb to the pressures, but to keep on adhering to sound doctrine and not to let anyone corrupt their churches. These are some good verses here, right, let's check out some more verses!

KJV-1 Timothy 1:6-7; **From which some having swerved have turned aside unto vain jangling; Desiring to be teachers of the law; understanding neither what they say, nor whereof they affirm.** Did you catch how it said **"understanding neither what they say"**?! So this verse is talking about pastors and or preachers who don't even really know what they talking about, you know, they just kinda making up stuff about the Bible thinking they are teaching truth but really they are clueless in their Biblical understanding!

KJV- 1 Timothy 6:3-14; **If any man teach otherwise, and consent not to wholesome words, *even* the words of our Lord Jesus Christ, and to the doctrine which is according to godliness;**

4 He is proud, knowing nothing, but doting about questions and strifes of words, whereof cometh envy, strife, railings, evil surmisings,

5 Perverse disputings of men of corrupt minds, and destitute of the truth, supposing that gain is godliness: from such withdraw thyself.

6 But godliness with contentment is great gain.

7 For we brought nothing into *this* world, *and it is* certain we can carry nothing out.

__8__ And having food and raiment let us be therewith content.

__9__ But they that will be rich fall into temptation and a snare, and *into* many foolish and hurtful lusts, which drown men in destruction and perdition.

__10__ For the love of money is the root of all evil: which while some coveted after, they have erred from the faith, and pierced themselves through with many sorrows.

__11__ But thou, O man of God, flee these things; and follow after righteousness, godliness, faith, love, patience, meekness.

__12__ Fight the good fight of faith, lay hold on eternal life, whereunto thou art also called, and hast professed a good profession before many witnesses.

__13__ I give thee charge in the sight of God, who quickeneth all things, and *before* Christ Jesus, who before Pontius Pilate witnessed a good confession;

__14__ **That thou keep *this* commandment without spot, unrebukeable, until the appearing of our Lord Jesus Christ:** This scripture right here is very powerful, did you get it, did you understand it!? Ok so, what this scripture is saying is, stay away from preachers with corrupt minds (**"Perverse disputings of men of corrupt minds"**), and who pervert the truth (**"and destitute of the truth"**), who teach that prosperity is godliness (**"supposing that gain is godliness"**). Wow, wow, wow, oh man, I feel sorry for all these prosperity gospel preachers! I also feel sorry for all these people that go to churches that teach prosperity as part of their doctrine, you know, that teach that God wants you to be rich.

I mean it's crazy, but it seems like a lot of churches nowadays mainly focus on what God can do for us here on earth, you know, what God can do for us as far as making us more prosperous down here on earth, you know what I mean? I mean, am I right or wrong!? I mean, come on, somebody talk to me, somebody say something, how have we gotten ourselves in such confusion over what the Bible says!? I mean, how and or why have we allowed ourselves to water down the Bible!? I mean, I just can't wrap my head around it, I just can't fathom how preachers would allow themselves to misguide their congregations with no regard to how they will have to answer to God for being bad shepherds. And this is why the Bible says that "many are called but few are chosen, you know, regarding becoming a preacher and or a pastor, you know what I mean!? And actually it seems like nowadays many preachers and or pastors just call themselves, you know, for whatever reason they think God is calling them to lead a church and or ministry but in actuality God didn't say a thing to them about that, and if they are not careful, it's probably the devil that is calling them to start a church and or ministry. And the reason why I say it's probably the devil that called them to be preachers and or pastors it's because, I truly refuse to believe that anybody that God calls and or choses to become a preacher and or pastor would be so unwise in the truth of the Word of God that they would allow themselves to water down God's word and teach what seems to feel good to their congregations instead of feeding them the true word of God, you know what I mean? And so therefore, preachers who teach false doctrines (whether consciously or subconsciously) must not really be called and or chosen by God, but instead they must have been called and or chosen by the devil, because I don't believe anybody that God calls and or choses to lead His flock would be so unwise to the true meaning of what the scriptures are saying.

I mean it's crazy, but there are a lot of preachers and or pastors that just don't seem to know what the heck they are talking about (in regards to the Bible), you know, they seem to just be making up stuff as they go, you know, feeding their congregations junk words, you know, useless words, you know what I mean!? And this is why the Bible says **"If any man teach otherwise, and consent not to wholesome words, *even* the words of our Lord Jesus Christ, and to the doctrine which is according to godliness; He is proud, knowing nothing, but doting about**

questions and strifes of words, whereof cometh envy, strife, railings, evil surmisings". Did you see that, did you see how it said **"He is proud, knowing nothing"**, wow, the Bible is no joke, it tells it like it is, right?! And this is why we must examine our churches and our pastors to make sure that they are teaching sound doctrine, because otherwise we can easily find ourselves being led astray from the true meaning of the scriptures. And so what I wanna do now, I want us to check out some scriptures that a lot of the prosperity gospel preaches might use to justify their prosperity doctrines. Are you ready, I'm ready, ok, let's get into the Bible?!

Ok, well, so, I tried to find some verses that prosperity gospel preachers might use to justify their prosperity doctrines, but I'm afraid to say that I had a hard time finding them. I mean, I did find a few that I think they might be using, but truth be told, I'm kinda disappointed that I didn't find a lot more. And the reason why I'm disappointed is because, if their whole prosperity gospel doctrine is based on these few verses that I found, then their false teaching is not based on just misinterpretation of these few scriptures, but their teaching is based mostly by their misunderstanding of the whole Bible as a whole. And the reason why I say this is because, the Bible is a spiritual book, and its main focus is not on matters of this (earthly) life, but on life after this, you know, eternal life. And so, to reduce the Bible and or God into the answer for our financial prosperity is to not understand what the Bible is all about completely. And notice how I said "completely", and the reason I said that is because the Bible is not really concerned about our physical condition here on earth, nope, it's really concerned about our spiritual condition here on earth, you know, it's concerned about us receiving salvation so we can have everlasting life up in Heaving, you know what I mean? I mean, let me try and re-explain what I mean, and what I mean is, the Bible is not worried about whether we live in a big house or a small house, the Bible is not worried about whether we live in a penthouse or a mud house, the Bible is not worried about whether we drive a nice car or a beat up car, the Bible is not worried whether we have a million dollar job or a minimum wage job, the Bible is not worried about whether we wear nice fancy clothes or worn out regular clothes, I mean, you get what I'm trying to say here!? And what I'm trying to say is, what the Bible cares about is your soul, not the condition of your earthly existence, the condition of your earthly existence is up to you, you know, that's why the Bible says: KJV-2 Thessalonians 3:8,10-12; **"Neither did we eat any man's bread for nought; but wrought with labour and travail night and day, that we might not be chargeable to any of you: For even when we were with you, this we commanded you, that if any would not work, neither should he eat. For we hear that there are some which walk among you disorderly, working not at all, but are busybodies. Now them that are such we command and exhort by our Lord Jesus Christ, that with quietness they work, and eat their own bread".** Ok, did you notice how it said: **"but wrought with labour and travail night and day"**, and **"that if any would not work, neither should he eat"**, and **"which walk among you disorderly, working not at all, but are busybodies"!** And what this means (to paraphrase) is, sometimes you gonna have to work extra hard to make ends meet, you know, laziness will not bring you any success, you gotta work hard for what you want, you know what I mean!? And so, the Bible is not really concerned about your earthly conditions, you know, it's not concerned whether your rich or poor, that will depend on your own will power, determination, preparation, focus, drive, sacrifice that you are willing to endure to achieve what you want to achieve in this life, you know, because God is only really concerned with your after life, and this is why He brought us Jesus, and it's so we could receive salvation, you know, no matter whether we are rich or poor.

And also this is why Jesus said: KJV-Matthew 26:11; **"For ye have the poor always with you; but me ye have not always".** And so this tells us that, not everyone is gonna be rich, you know, there always gonna be poor people, and so, to suggest that we were all meant to be rich because we are saved is terribly false, because if that was the case, this would mean that most of us who believe we are saved, it would mean that even though we are save, it would mean our faith is not sufficient enough for God to bless us with financial prosperity, and if that is the case, then it would mean that most of us who believe we are saved are not really saved at all, you know, because otherwise there's no reason why we are not rich already if our faith is sufficient enough for salvation, then it should be sufficient enough for God to make us rich. I mean, I'm sorry I'm not doing a good job of explaining what I mean, but, just think about it, why would God grant us salvation if our faith in Jesus Christ is not sufficient? And so, to suggest that the reason why most of us are not rich is because our faith in Christ is not strong enough, and or, the reason why God is not granting us financial prosperity is because we are not doing a good job of asking Him (in prayer), and or the reason why God is not showering us with financial blessings is because we are not doing a good job of sowing our seeds (paying tithes), if these are the reasons, these reasons are a terrible misrepresentation of God and His word (the Bible).

    I mean it's crazy, but millions of Christians are allowing themselves to be deceived and or lead astray from what God and the Bible is all about. I mean, these prosperity gospel preachers have actually succeeded in getting millions of Christians to think that if they wanna be rich all they gotta do is either pray harder and or pay more tithe to their churches and or ministries. I mean it's crazy how these preachers have succeeded in getting millions of Christians to think of God like the stock market and the Bible like the financial advisory report, you know what I mean!? And what I mean is, these preachers have gotten millions of Christians to think that the main reason for going to church and worshipping God is so in return God can grant them with great financial blessings, you know what I mean? I mean it's crazy, but I have always wondered how and or why are these preachers so able to manipulate their congregations like that, you know, to where some church members actually go broke trying to keep up with paying tithes and stuff, you know, because they are afraid that if they don't pay tithe there's no way that God will grant them any financial blessings, you know, when in actuality paying tithe has nothing to do with sowing your seeds, paying tithe is a free will that you do so as to help foster the churches financial ability to meet its expenses as it works to minister the Word of God where ever it can. And so, if you ain't got no money to give and or you only got just a little bit of money you can give, that's fine, God is not gonna hold that against you. But also, if you do have a bunch of money that you can give, by all means do so, but just remember, just because you are giving a lot of money doesn't mean that your money is worth more in God's eyes than the person who can only give a just a little bit, because in God's eyes, it's not about who gives the most money, it's about who gives with an open and or pure heart, which means, they are giving all they can give and they are doing so without the expectation that God will bless them with more money as a result.

And so yeah, prosperity gospel is a false doctrine, and if you are a member of a church that practices prosperity gospel it's bet's you flee from there as soon as you can, because all your worshipping and or praying will be corrupted by the false doctrine which will hinder your personal relationship with God, you know, because instead of praising and thanking Him for the blessing of salvation that He gave to you freely (through Jesus Christ), you will instead be praising and thanking Him for some financial blessings that you are praying He will bless you with sooner than later because of your strong faith in Jesus Christ (see how twisted that thinking is). And so this is one of the reasons why I named this book "Christianity Lost", and it's because there's just too many Christians out there who are lost, you know, whether it's because of their own laziness in not trying to read the Bible and understand what it really says, or it's because they belong in churches that have corrupted their minds to where they become blind to the falsehood that their churches are teaching them, you know, they have become so comfortable with the doctrine that their churches teaches that they can't even imagine to think that their churches might actually not be teaching sound doctrine, you know what I mean?

Ok, so, before we conclude this chapter (on doctrine), I want us to check out these few scriptures that I found that I think prosperity gospel preachers tend to use to justify their prosperity gospel teaching. Now, I'm sure there's probably more scriptures that prosperity gospel preachers might use than the ones I found, if so, please feel free to send them to me so I can check them out, because I'm here to learn truth, thereby I wouldn't want to miss any scripture that might be able to correct my understanding of the Bible as a whole, you know, as we compare scripture with scripture so we can discern the real truth of the meaning of the verses. Ok, let's check out some scriptures!

KJV- John 10:10; **"The thief cometh not, but for to steal, and to kill, and to destroy: I am come that they might have life, and that they might have *it* more abundantly."** I think this is one of the verses that prosperity gospel preachers use to justify their prosperity gospel, you know, thinking that when Jesus says **"I am come that they might have life, and that they might have *it* more abundantly"**, they think that Jesus was talking about more abundant life here on earth, when in actuality Jesus was talking about more abundant life up in Heaven, you know, Jesus was talking about everlasting life, eternal life, you know, it has nothing to do with being rich here on earth, you know what I mean!? That was an easy one to explain, because the whole deal with Jesus coming to earth was not so He could make us rich, oh no, not at all, He came so we could receive salvation through Him, thereby giving us eternal life (abundant life) up in Heaven. Ok, did you get it, did my explanation make sense, yeah I think you got it, let's check out some more scriptures!

KJV- James 4:2-3; **"Ye lust, and have not: ye kill, and desire to have, and cannot obtain: ye fight and war, yet ye have not, because ye ask not. Ye ask, and receive not, because ye ask amiss, that ye may consume *it* upon your lusts".** Now, these verses were kinda of a little bit tricky to discern, I mean, I had to re-read them a few times more and I had to read a few verses that came before them and read a few verses that came after them in trying to understand what they were really trying to say to us. But it didn't take me that long to get it, and what they are saying is that, the reason why we ask God to bless us with something and we don't receive it is because we are asking for the wrong things. And what I mean by we asking for the wrong things is, instead of asking for things like; wisdom, strength, health, will power, motivation, grace, forgiveness, and so on, we instead ask for things like; houses, cars, money and so on, you know, we are asking for things that will bring us instant gratification instead of asking for things that will give us the strength and or wisdom to improve our lives here on earth while striving to be better Christians. And how I came to this understanding is, you see how it says **"Ye ask,** and receive not, because ye ask amiss, that ye may consume *it* upon your lusts,"** well the word amiss here means "wrong", and so combine it with "that ye may consume it upon your lusts", this makes amiss to mean "wrong things", and the reason I say this is because "that ye may consume it" can only mean so we can use it, "upon your lusts", means for our material pleasures! Man, I hope you got all of that, because I don't feel like re-explaining it, because it was kind of exhausting, you know, trying to break it down to its core just kind of exhausted me right now, lol. You know what, this is probably the reason why a lot of people tend to easily misinterpret the Bible, and it's because some verses require extra examination, you know, some verses actually will require you to break down almost every word in the phrase, you know, so as to make sure that you don't miss any word that could potentially make you misunderstand the true meaning of the verse. But, that's the Bible for you, you gotta have a lot of patience when reading it, otherwise you can easily misinterpret it, which you don't wanna do. Ok, let's check out some more verses! Ahm, actually, the last verse has kinda of completely worn me out for tonight, I mean, I was already kinda tired, but the last verse has just totally finished me off for tonight, and my eyes have started to close by themselves right about now, so I wanna bid you "usiku mwema" (that means good night in Swahili), and we'll get back to this captivating Bible study again tomorrow, God willing, Amen!

Alright, good morning, I just crashed about five hours of sleep, I'm feeling pretty rested and ready to get back to our Bible study, so come on, let's get back to it!

KJV- Philippians 4:5-7; **Let your moderation be known unto all men. The Lord *is* at hand.**

6 Be careful for nothing; but in every thing by prayer and supplication with thanksgiving let your requests be made known unto God.

7 And the peace of God, which passeth all understanding, shall keep your hearts and minds through Christ Jesus. Ok, I think verse 6 of this scripture is another verse that prosperity gospel preachers tend to use to justify what they teach, you know, the part that says **"but in every thing by prayer and supplication with thanksgiving let your requests be made known unto God"**. And so, what I have done here, I have listed verses 5 and 7 so you can see how the verse before and the verse after the main verse can help in explaining the verse that you are trying to discern the true meaning of it. And so, see how verse 5 says **"Let your moderation be known unto all men"**, moderation in this verse pretty much means either modesty or humbleness. And then, you see how verse 6 says **"Be careful for nothing"**, this pretty much means don't worry about anything. And see how verse 7 says **"And the peace of God, which passeth all understanding, shall keep your hearts and minds through Christ Jesus"**, this verse pretty much means that; the greatness of God, which is more than we can comprehend, will bring us strength and comfort through Christ Jesus. And so the part where it says **"but in every thing by prayer and supplication with thanksgiving let your requests be made known unto God"**, that part pretty much means, in whatever situation you might find yourself in, pray on it with the assurance that God will see you through it, you know, ask God to handle the issues that seem to be too much for you to handle, and do so with prayer and thankfulness, knowing that God can help us go through any situation. And so as you can see, verse 6 has really nothing to do with material needs, nope, it's pretty much dealing with our mental needs, you know, like strength, comfort, motivation, focus, wisdom, and so on, you know what I mean!? Ok, I got one more scripture that I wanna check out on this prosperity thing!

KJV- Mark 10:17-30; **And when he was gone forth into the way, there came one running, and kneeled to him, and asked him, Good Master, what shall I do that I may inherit eternal life?**

18 And Jesus said unto him, Why callest thou me good? *there is* **none good but one,** *that is*, **God.**

19 Thou knowest the commandments, Do not commit adultery, Do not kill, Do not steal, Do not bear false witness, Defraud not, Honour thy father and mother.

20 And he answered and said unto him, Master, all these have I observed from my youth.

21 Then Jesus beholding him loved him, and said unto him, One thing thou lackest: go thy way, sell whatsoever thou hast, and give to the poor, and thou shalt have treasure in heaven: and come, take up the cross, and follow me.

22 And he was sad at that saying, and went away grieved: for he had great possessions.

23 And Jesus looked round about, and saith unto his disciples, How hardly shall they that have riches enter into the kingdom of God!

24 And the disciples were astonished at his words. But Jesus answereth again, and saith unto them, Children, how hard is it for them that trust in riches to enter into the kingdom of God!

25 It is easier for a camel to go through the eye of a needle, than for a rich man to enter into the kingdom of God.

26 And they were astonished out of measure, saying among themselves, Who then can be saved?

27 And Jesus looking upon them saith, With men *it is* impossible, but not with God: for with God all things are possible.

28 Then Peter began to say unto him, Lo, we have left all, and have followed thee.

29 And Jesus answered and said, Verily I say unto you, There is no man that hath left house, or brethren, or sisters, or father, or mother, or wife, or children, or lands, for my sake, and the gospel's,

30 But he shall receive an hundredfold now in this time, houses, and brethren, and sisters, and mothers, and children, and lands, with persecutions; and in the world to come eternal life. Ok, so, this verse (verse 30) is another verse that prosperity gospel preachers like to use to justify their prosperity gospel doctrine. And the part that says **"But he shall receive an hundredfold now in this time"**, this is the phrase that the prosperity preachers like to use to tell their followers that they can receive a great deal of financial blessing if they faithfully ask God for it, which is false, that's not what the verse is saying. And what the verse is really saying is, anybody that dedicates their life to Christ and the Word of God instead of houses, land or family will receive a lot more houses, land or family now in this time (with mistreatment), and eternal life in the world to come. Did you get it, did you understand it, no, not really, yeah I don't think I did a good job of explaining it, so let me try to explain it again?!

Ok so, you see how it says **"But he shall receive an hundredfold"**, well, that hundredfold does not actually mean a hundred times more, no, it more so means many more or a lot more. And then, you see how it says **"houses, and brethren, and sisters, and mothers, and children, and lands"**, well, this more so means family with houses and land. And then, you see how it says **"with persecutions"**, well, this pretty much means with mistreatment. And then finally, you see how it says **"and in the world to come eternal life"**, well, this means salvation. And then so, if we put all the meanings together, what we get is; anybody that dedicates their life to serving Christ and the Word of God instead of family and houses and land will receive a lot more family members and houses and land. But, they will experience a lot of mistreatment as they work to serve Christ and promote the Word of God. But, they will also receive salvation (eternal life).

Now, you are probably asking yourself, how are you gonna receive more houses, family and land, or, you are probably asking yourself, does this mean that you gonna personally receive a whole lot of houses, family and land, right!? Well, the answer is no, you are not personally gonna receive a lot more houses, family and land, no, you not gonna receive these things personally, but you are gonna receive these things inclusively, that is, you gonna receive these things inclusively with the other believers and or the other church members. Ok, let me explain it better, and what I mean is, as you dedicate your life to Christ, you gonna be a member of the body of Christ right here on earth, as in, you either gonna be a member of a church, or you gonna be associated with other Christians who have also dedicated their lives to serving Christ. And so, as a member of a church, or as a dedicated Christian, those other members of your church, or those other dedicated Christians actually become your brothers and sisters in Christ, you know what I mean? And so it's like, these your fellow Christians become your family in Christ, you know, the mothers in the church become your mothers, the fathers in the church become your fathers, the children in the church become your children, and the brothers and sisters in the church become your brothers and sisters. And then so, since the church members become your family, not only does this mean that you have gained a lot more fathers, mothers, sisters, brothers, and children, but this will mean that you have also gained a lot of houses, and or land. Now, you are probably asking, how have you gained a lot of houses and or land, well, since these church members are now your family, this means that their houses and lands are also yours. And what I mean by this is, it's like, the way we Christians are really supposed to live our lives is by taking care of each other, as in, we are supposed to share our resources (financial and or material things, such as houses, land, etc.,), you know, we are supposed to look out for each other, you know, like (for example), if a church member loses their job and or doesn't have a place to stay, another church member is supposed to take that person in and let them stay at their house until the person finds another job and gets themselves back on their feet, you know what I mean? And so, this is what Jesus meant when He said you will receive a lot more houses, which meant, you will have a lot of houses where you can stay at, you know, because as a part of the body of Christ, anything a Christian owns (houses, land, cars, money, etc.) does not just belong to himself or herself, no, it really belongs to the body of Christ, which is the people of God. I mean, are you kinda understanding what I'm trying to say here, I mean, I know I'm getting extra deep with it, but are you kinda getting it!? I hope you are kinda getting it, because this verse is actually pretty deep, which I don't think most people are really ready to go that deep with it, but, you know what, I will re-visit this part in a later chapter called "Follow Me", which I'm gonna use to go extra deep in discussing what being a Christian is all about!

But so anyway, verse 30 has nothing to do with getting a lot of money if you faithfully ask God for it, nope, not at all. And one way you can be sure that it has nothing to do with money is by comparing the verses before it, you know, so you can get the full context of the conversation that lead to this verse. And this is why I provided a bunch of other verses that comes before verse 30, this way you can read and see for yourself what led to Jesus giving this verse. And as you read the preceding verses, pay close attention to how Jesus warns us about the dangers of being rich. And actually, what I wanna do now, I wanna go ahead and list a few more scriptures that talk about the dangers of chasing money and or riches, you know, so you can read and see for yourself that there's no way that God would be in the business of trying to make people rich, when He already knows that money can greatly lead us astray from Him, you know, as we focus more on our riches than on our spirituality. And so, here are some scriptures that I would like for you to check out: KJV-Matthew 6:19-21, 24; **Lay not up for yourselves treasures upon earth, where moth and rust doth corrupt, and where thieves break through and steal:**

20 But lay up for yourselves treasures in heaven, where neither moth nor rust doth corrupt, and where thieves do not break through nor steal:

21 For where your treasure is, there will your heart be also.

24 No man can serve two masters: for either he will hate the one, and love the other; or else he will hold to the one, and despise the other. Ye cannot serve God and mammon.

KJV-Colossians 3:2-3; **"Set your affection on things above, not on things on the earth".**

KJV- Ecclesiastes 5:9-20; **Moreover the profit of the earth is for all: the king *himself* is served by the field.**

<u>10</u> He that loveth silver shall not be satisfied with silver; nor he that loveth abundance with increase: this *is* also vanity.

<u>11</u> When goods increase, they are increased that eat them: and what good *is there* to the owners thereof, saving the beholding *of them* with their eyes?

<u>12</u> The sleep of a labouring man *is* sweet, whether he eat little or much: but the abundance of the rich will not suffer him to sleep.

<u>13</u> There is a sore evil *which* I have seen under the sun, *namely*, riches kept for the owners thereof to their hurt.

<u>14</u> But those riches perish by evil travail: and he begetteth a son, and *there is* nothing in his hand.

<u>15</u> As he came forth of his mother's womb, naked shall he return to go as he came, and shall take nothing of his labour, which he may carry away in his hand.

<u>16</u> And this also *is* a sore evil, *that* in all points as he came, so shall he go: and what profit hath he that hath laboured for the wind?

<u>17</u> All his days also he eateth in darkness, and *he hath* much sorrow and wrath with his sickness.

<u>18</u> Behold *that* which I have seen: *it is* good and comely *for one* to eat and to drink, and to enjoy the good of all his labour that he

taketh under the sun all the days of his life, which God giveth him: for it *is* his portion.

<u>19</u> Every man also to whom God hath given riches and wealth, and hath given him power to eat thereof, and to take his portion, and to rejoice in his labour; this *is* the gift of God.

<u>20</u> For he shall not much remember the days of his life; because God answereth *him* in the joy of his heart.

KJV-Hebrews 13:5; **"Let your conversation be without covetousness; and be content with such things as ye have: for he hath said, I will never leave thee, nor forsake thee".**

Ok, so, what do you think, are you convinced yet that God is not in the business of trying to make people rich. And actually to tell you the truth, I don't really think there's anything wrong with being rich, it's just that there's so much danger in it, you know, it's so much easy for a person to lose themselves in their riches and forget all about God, you know what I mean? And so, I don't really think being rich is in its self a sin, I believe that being rich can greatly cause us to become sinners, whether consciously or not, you know, whether by commission or by omission. And what I mean by commission and or omission is; the sin of commission is the sin that we actively commit, you know, like; stealing, lying, cheating, and so on. And the sin of omission is the sin that we don't actively do, you know, like; not feeding the hungry, not sheltering the homeless, not obeying the commandments, and so on. And this is why Jesus said **"It is easier for a camel to go through the eye of a needle, than for a rich man to enter into the kingdom of God"**. And the reason why He said this is because, He knows that the heart of a rich person tends to be corrupt to where instead of focusing on their spirituality and God they would rather focus on getting even richer and enjoy the things of this world, you know, like (for example) instead of spending their money on spreading the gospel, they would rather spend their money on buying mansions, or, instead of spending their money on sheltering the homeless, they would rather spend their money on buying yachts, or, instead of spending their money to feed the hungry, they would rather spend their money on buying a collection of fancy cars, and so on and so on. I mean, it's like, with the amount of rich people that there are in this world (with a lot of them being Christians), there should not be this much hunger and misery in the world, because I mean, truth be told, there's actually more than enough natural resources in this would to actually eradicate hunger in the world. But, what's happening is, the rich do not want to share their resources with the poor, you know, the rich refuse to share and or allow natural resources to be equally available to people who do not have enough financial ability to acquire these natural resources so as to help themselves climb up the financial ladder. I mean, I'm hoping you are understanding what I'm trying to say here, because I have really thought about this rich and poor thing, you know, I have really thought about the reason why the rich seem to be forever getting richer and why the poor seem to forever getting poorer. And it's all because of the unwillingness for the rich to want to share the earth's resources with the poor, and the reason why they don't want to share the earth's resources with the poor is because of their greed, you know, their greed to accumulate even more wealth for themselves and their own families, you know, without regard for the rest of their fellow human beings.

Anyway, it is what it is, but I truly believe that if Christians (especially the rich ones) really knew what it really means to be a Christian, I truly believe this world would be a better world. And the reason why I say this is because, there's enough rich Christians out there that can greatly make a major impact in the world today, especially with all these major disasters that are going on around the world, you know, from earthquakes, to hurricanes, to wars, to famines, and so on and on. And this is why the Bible says "to whom much is given much is required", and it's because there's always gonna be less fortunate people around the world, for whatever reason. And so, for this world to be a better place, we all have to chip in to help alleviate whatever struggles others might unfortunately find themselves in, you know, for no fault of their own.

Ok, oh man, I didn't mean to go on a tirade, my apology, but I just shake my head at how inhuman we humans tend to treat each other most often than not, you know what I mean!? But so anyway, yeah, being rich can greatly corrupt a person's heart to where their life becomes all about them, and all about their riches, to where their spirituality ends up taking a back seat and or taking a hike, you know what I mean? And this is why the Bible strongly warns about chasing riches, and this is why the prosperity gospel doctrine is false, and it's because God is not concerned about us being rich or not, He is concerned about us receiving eternal life. Now, God can grant us favor, to where we can end up becoming rich, but if He does, it won't be because we been faithfully asking Him to, no, not at all, it will be because of His own reasoning and choosing. I mean, I'm sure you have heard the saying that God is not a respecter of persons, you know, meaning that He will chose whom He wants to choose, you know, it don't matter a person's standing in life, you know, upper class or lower class, or whatever, nope, God will chose to grant favor to whom He wishes to grant favor, and it's His own reasoning and or purpose. Now, before we conclude on this chapter (for the second time, lol), there's one more scripture that I want us to check out, which talks about God blessing someone with riches, let's check it out! KJV-1 Kings 3:5-13; **In Gibeon the LORD appeared to Solomon in a dream by night: and God said, Ask what I shall give thee.**

6 And Solomon said, Thou hast shewed unto thy servant David my father great mercy, according as he walked before thee in truth, and in righteousness, and in uprightness of heart with thee; and thou hast kept for him this great kindness, that thou hast given him a son to sit on his throne, as *it is* this day.

7 And now, O LORD my God, thou hast made thy servant king instead of David my father: and I *am but* a little child: I know not *how* to go out or come in.

__8__ And thy servant *is* in the midst of thy people which thou hast chosen, a great people, that cannot be numbered nor counted for multitude.

__9__ Give therefore thy servant an understanding heart to judge thy people, that I may discern between good and bad: for who is able to judge this thy so great a people?

__10__ And the speech pleased the Lord, that Solomon had asked this thing.

__11__ And God said unto him, Because thou hast asked this thing, and hast not asked for thyself long life; neither hast asked riches for thyself, nor hast asked the life of thine enemies; but hast asked for thyself understanding to discern judgment;

__12__ Behold, I have done according to thy words: lo, I have given thee a wise and an understanding heart; so that there was none like thee before thee, neither after thee shall any arise like unto thee.

__13__ And I have also given thee that which thou hast not asked, both riches, and honour: so that there shall not be any among the kings like unto thee all thy days.

Ok, wow, did you see that, did you see how God asked Solomon to ask for what he wants, and did you see how Solomon instead of asking for money, did you see how he asked for wisdom. And then so, did you see how God was so pleased that Solomon asked for wisdom instead of money, and then did you see how God ended up blessing Solomon with money anyway, you know, that's what I'm talking about, God can grant you favor, and it won't be because you asked for it, it will be because He wants to, you know, for His own reasoning and or purpose. And so this is why the prosperity gospel doctrine is false, God will not grant you financial blessing because you asked for it faithfully, nah, He will grant you financial blessing if He chooses to according to His own purpose. And

I mean, God already knows what situations we are going through on a daily basis, and so He already said He won't forsake us if we put our trust in Him, and so, if it's His will that we become rich (for whatever reason), than that will happen, but if it's not His will for us to become rich, then it won't happen, not from His blessing anyways, you know what I mean? And what I mean by not from His blessing is, not everyone who becomes rich is by the blessing of God, you know, there's a lot of people who become rich by other means, you know, like (for example) by cheating, stealing, manipulation, embezzling, and so on, you know, by wicked means, not by honesty. And so anyway, yeah, prosperity gospel is not Biblical, it's pretty much man made, and most often times it serves to benefit the preachers and not the congregations, as you can see with the rise of the megachurches!

I mean it's crazy, but there are a lot of Christians who attend churches that do not teach and or do not practice sound doctrine, you know, their teachings don't really align with what the Bible actually teaches, which is a shame. So it is very important to make sure that your church is teaching and or practicing sound doctrine, that way your spiritual growth is not limited. And so to conclude, if you find yourself in one of these churches (that don't teach sound doctrine), and if you try to raise the issues that you find to be un Biblical but your church leaders refuse to correct them, then it's best you flee from that church and either go find another church that seems to be more Biblical, or, you might just have to go and start your own church, you know, so other people who are looking for a true Bible worshipping and teaching church will have somewhere to go and fellowship with other Bible adhering Christians. Oh, before we conclude again (for the third time, lol), I just got two more verses that I want to leave with you, if you don't mind!

KJV-2 Timothy 3:16; **All scripture *is* given by inspiration of God, and *is* profitable for doctrine, for reproof, for correction, for instruction in righteousness:**

KJV-2 Timothy 1:13; **Hold fast the form of sound words, which thou hast heard of me, in faith and love which is in Christ Jesus.**

Ok my friends, or should I say, ok my brothers and sisters in the Lord, that's it for this chapter, I hope it was enlightening, and don't be afraid to flee from your church if you find that they are not teaching sound doctrine!

5

SPEAKING IN TONGUES

When I was about 11 years old (back in Africa), I heard that there was an American preacher in my town, I think he was there for a revival or something like that. I don't really remember about it that much, but I remember they were saying that he was healing people and casting out demons and stuff like that. And so being the curious young kid that I was, I decided to go over to the church that this thing was taking place and see it for myself. The church was about 45 minutes from where I lived. So on that weekend (I think it was a Saturday), around the evening time, I put on my sandals and did the 45 minute walk to the church (by myself, I was kind of a loner when I was younger, well, truth be told, I'm still kind of a loner even today, at my adult age, lol). And so when I got to the church, I started seeing and hearing people shouting, yelling, screaming and stuff like that, you know, saying hallelujah, thank you Lord, and so on. And they were saying these things in Swahili, which is my native language. And then, as I got closer to the stage (they had a small stage set up outside of the church), I saw the preacher putting his hands on people and speaking in a language that I couldn't understand. The whole thing was just so fascinating to me, I mean, the whole excitement of the people, and him on stage laying hands on the people that were on the stage, and the people being healed of whatever sickness and or physical disabilities they might have had (now whether they were being healed for real or just faking it I'm not sure, but I did hear rumors of fakeness tending to happen in these kind of events, but I withhold my judgement, because you just never know), and the people shouting in excitement was just so fascinating to me. And the reason why it was so fascinating to me is because, I had never really seen people that excited about worshipping and praising God, you know, because at my church we were pretty subdued at our services. I mean, we weren't as subdued and or boring as Catholic services, lol (which I have attended a few times), but we definitely were never as animated as the people were at that church.

And so as I stood there watching what was going on, I became fascinated with this strange language that I had never heard before. I mean, my native language is Swahili, and most the people there were pretty much worshipping and praising God in Swahili, so I could pretty much understand what they were saying. But, there were other people that were shouting and praising God in a strange language, I mean, it wasn't English, and it wasn't any of the other languages that the people in my country spoke, because if they were, I would have been able to at least detect the dialect and or accent and be able to predict which tribe and or village they were from, you know what I mean? And so I was very fascinated with this strange language, but I just couldn't place it. But so anyway, when the whole thing was over (as it started to get dark), they separated all the men, women and children and had us sit in kind of a circle on the grass and they started to bring out some food for everybody. So I went ahead sat down, washed my hands and proceeded to feed my face to the max, lol. And the food was real good too, I mean, I can still taste it even now today about 30 years later, ha ha ha ha ha!

But anyway, after I ate, I started my walk back home, hoping to get there before it got extra dark and my folks start to really worry about my where bouts. I remember as I was walking, I remember thinking about that strange language that I had heard at the church, I thought about it all the way home, but I still could not place it, and I never heard it again until about 12 years later when I was in the United States Army stationed at Fort Hood, Texas. And what had happened was, one day me and one of my fellow soldiers were talking about either the Bible or Christianity, I can't really remember what exactly we were talking about, but he ended up inviting me to the church he was attending. And so I agreed to go that following Sunday, that is, if I didn't party too hard that Saturday night, you know what I mean, lol. I mean, you see, at this period in my life (that young adulthood period), partying on Friday and Saturday nights (that club life) was the norm, you know, and to add to that being in the military, forget about it, I mean, you know how soldiers party, right, lol.

But so anyway, when the following Sunday came, I was ready for church. I don't remember if I partied hard that Saturday night before hand or not, but that Sunday morning I was ready and eager to go to church, especially since I hadn't been to church in a while after I joined the military. So he came and picked me up and we drove to the church. The church was not that for from the base, se we got there in no time at all. The church was kinda smallish, but it looked nice inside and had pretty good energy to it. And so as we walked in, people were already singing and clapping their hands, we had gotten there just a few minutes after the service had started. So we went ahead and found were to sit and joined in the singing and hand clapping. I probably did not know the songs, so I probably did more hand clapping than singing, lol, you know what I mean? The rest of the service went well, I enjoyed myself, but, I couldn't really handle all the crying that was taking place that went along with the excitement, you know, as people shouted out hallelujah, Amen and something else using that same strange language that I hadn't heard of since I was about 11 years old. Yup, yes, that's right, that strange language that I had heard when I was 11 years old at that church in Africa, I finally heard it again about 12 years later in America. And so as you can imagine, I spent most of that church service just fascinated the way the people were shouting out something in this strange language that I hadn't heard in years, a language that I still couldn't understand. And so after the service, as me and my fellow army soldier were driving back to base, I asked him about that strange language that some of the people were shouting out at the service. And this is when I first came to find out that the strange language is called "speaking in tongues". I don't remember if I asked him any more questions about it, but I never went back to that church, and it wasn't because of the "speaking in tongues" thing, no, it was more because I just wasn't used to all that emotion going on in the service, you know, the yelling, the shouting, the crying, and so on, you know, I'm used to more subdued church services, you know what I mean, lol.

And so anyway, as time went on I kept hearing about speaking in tongues here and there, and I came to understand that it is supposed to mean the evidence of a person's salvation, you know, it's the gift of utterance that a person receives when they get saved and get filled with the Holy Ghost. It's a very fascinating theology, and I used to wonder why I never heard about it from any of my churches that I used to attend. But nevertheless, even though I was curious about it, I never really tried to find out if it was true or not, you know, by searching out the Bible, but I was very skeptical about it. And the reason why I was skeptical is because, if speaking in tongues was really the evidence of a person's salvation, then a lot more denominations would have this practice as part of their doctrine, but instead this practice is only observed by a few (mostly Pentecostal & Apostolic churches) denominations. Now, don't get me wrong, I don't mean to suggest that just because the majority of Christians don't practice a doctrine means that a doctrine is false, oh no, what I'm saying is, if the doctrine is true, then a lot more Christians would want to practice it, you know what I mean? And the reason why I say this is because, if indeed speaking in tongue is the evidence of a Christians' salvation, I don't see how any Christian would pass up on a chance to receive this evidence, you know, because as humans, there's nothing more we trust then something we can physically see and or feel, you know what I mean? And so this is why I was very skeptical about the speaking in tongues doctrine, and it's because I just couldn't see how any Christian would want to pass up on it, you know, which led me to believe that it was most likely a misinterpretation of the Bible.

And so, I never really worried too much about the speaking in tongues practice, that is until about five years ago when I decided to start reading the Bible a lot more seriously. And what happened was, as I was reading the Bible, I kept running into verses that had the words tongue or tongues in them. And so one day I decided maybe I should search out the whole Bible and see what it had to say about speaking in tongues, you know, and see if it's really Biblical or not. And so what I did was, I went ahead and searched out all the verses that had the words tongue or tongues in them, and then I worked on discerning each verse to see if it said anything about speaking in tongues being the evidence of a person's salvation. I don't remember how long it took me to go through all the verses, but I do remember that most of the verses were not that hard to discern, because most of the verses were pretty straight forward in what the meaning of tongues in those verses meant. I did find about two or three verses that did give me pause, you know, they made me take extra time and double or triple check them so as to make sure that I had the true meaning of them. And I think these are the verses that people who believe in speaking in tongues use to justify their doctrine. But so, after I finished going over all the verses, I'm afraid to say that I did not find any verses that confirmed that speaking in tongues was the evidence of a person's salvation. And actually, I ended up finding a few verses that not only contradicts how speaking in tongues is supposed to be used, but I also found a verse that actually said that speaking in tongues is not even the greatest gift of the Holy Ghost, you know, it's one of the lesser gifts of the Holy Ghost. I remember when I read that verse my mouth just kinda dropped, you know, because I'm thinking, how could the evidence of a person's salvation not be the greatest gift of the Holy Ghost. And the reason why I say this is because, the Bible and the reason why Christ came to earth is so we can receive salvation, you know, so why would the Bible say that speaking in tongues is not even the greatest of the gifts of the Holy Ghost if it is the evidence of us receiving salvation, I mean, you see what I'm saying!? And so that verse and the other verses that seem to contradict how speaking in tongues was supposed to be used finally made me understand what speaking in tongues really means, and it does not mean what the people who believe in speaking in tongues think it means, which makes their doctrine false, you know, they have totally misinterpreted the verses, which is very sad. And the reason why it is very sad is because, there are millions of Christians who actually totally believe in speaking in tongues, you know, they totally believe in it, they totally believe in a doctrine that is not Biblical, which means that they are lost, which is very sad, you know what I mean!?

And so, what I wanna do now, I want us to go into the Bible and check out every verse that has the word tongue or tongues in them and examine the true meaning of each verse. And the reason I wanna do that is because, I don't want you to just take my words for it, you know, I want you to actually read the verses for yourself and see if my explanation of the verses actually make sense, you know what I mean? Ok so, are you ready to get into the Bible and do some due diligence in examining these verses? You are, you ready, ok cool, let's do it!

KJV-Genesis 10:5; **"By these were the isles of the Gentiles divided in their lands; every one after his tongue, after their families, in their nations."** Ok, so tongue on this verse pretty much means language, as it says; the Gentiles were separated into their own nations and each nation spoke their own language. So tongue does not mean evidence of salvation on this verse!

KJV-Genesis 10:20; **"These are the sons of Ham, after their families, after their tongues, in their countries, and in their nations."** So tongues on this verse also means language, as it says; they spoke their own language in their own nation. So tongues does not mean evidence of salvation on this verse!

KJV-Genesis 10:31; **"These are the sons of Shem, after their families, after their tongues, in their lands, after their nations."** So tongues on this verse also means language, as it says; they had their own language and their own nation. So tongues does not mean evidence of salvation on this verse!

KJV-Exodus 4:10; **"And Moses said unto the LORD, O my Lord, I am not eloquent, neither heretofore, nor since thou hast spoken unto thy servant: but I am slow of speech, and of a slow tongue."** So tongue on this verse also means language, as Moses tells God that he is not articulate enough, and he is not much of a talker, and he's not too fancy with words. So tongue does not mean evidence of salvation on this verse!

KJV-Exodus 11:7; **"But against any of the children of Israel shall not a dog move his tongue, against man or beast: that ye may know how that the LORD doth put a difference between the Egyptians and Israel."** Ok, so I had to double check on this one, but it looks like tongue on this verse means mouth, as it says; not a dog move his tongue, which can only mean no dog will open their mouth to bite. So tongue does not mean evidence of salvation on this verse!

KJV-Deuteronomy 28:49; **"The LORD shall bring a nation against thee from far, from the end of the earth, as swift as the eagle flieth; a nation whose tongue thou shalt not understand."** So tongue on this verse means language, as it says; a nation whose language you will not understand. So tongue does not mean evidence of salvation on this verse!

KJV-Joshua 10:21; **"And all the people returned to the camp to Joshua at Makkedah in peace: none moved his tongue against any of the children of Israel."** So tongue on this verse means speaking, as it says; no one said anything against any of the children of Israel. So tongue does not mean evidence of salvation on this verse!

KJV-Judges 7:5; **"So he brought down the people unto the water: and the LORD said unto Gideon, Every one that lappeth of the water with his tongue, as a dog lappeth, him shalt thou set by himself; likewise every one that boweth down upon his knees to drink."** So tongue on this verse actually means tongue, you know, like the tongue in your mouth. So tongue does not mean evidence of salvation on this verse!

KJV-2 Samuel 23:2; **"The Spirit of the LORD spake by me, and his word was in my tongue."** So tongue on this verse actually means speech or talk, as in, he knew the word of God well enough to speak and or talk about it. So tongue does not mean evidence of salvation on this verse!

KJV-Ezra 4:7; **"And in the days of Artaxerxes wrote Bishlam, Mithredath, Tabeel, and the rest of their companions, unto Artaxerxes king of Persia; and the writing of the letter was written in the Syrian tongue, and interpreted in the Syrian tongue."** So tongue on this verse pretty much means language, as it says; the letter was written in the Syrian tongue (language), and interpreted in the Syrian tongue (language). So tongue does not mean evidence of salvation on this verse!

KJV-Esther 7:4; **"For we are sold, I and my people, to be destroyed, to be slain, and to perish. But if we had been sold for bondmen and bondwomen, I had held my tongue, although the enemy could not countervail the king's damage."** So tongue on this verse pretty much means speech or talk, as it says; I had held my tongue, which means she didn't say anything, right!? So tongue does not mean evidence of salvation on this verse!

KJV-Job 5:21; **"Thou shalt be hid from the scourge of the tongue: neither shalt thou be afraid of destruction when it cometh."** So tongue on this verse means speech or talk, as it says; scourge of the tongue, which is like saying lashing of the tongue, you know what I mean? So tongue does not mean evidence of salvation on this verse!

KJV-Job 6:24; **"Teach me, and I will hold my tongue: and cause me to understand wherein I have erred."** So tongue on this verse means speech or talk, as it says; I will hold my tongue, which means, he will not talk back but listen. So tongue does not mean evidence of salvation on this verse!

KJV-Job 6:30; **"Is there iniquity in my tongue? cannot my taste discern perverse things?"** So tongue on this verse actually means just that, tongue, as it says; cannot my taste discern perverse things, and what do we taste things with, it's by our tongues, right!?. So tongue does not mean evidence of salvation on this verse!

KJV-Job 13:19; **"Who is he that will plead with me? for now, if I hold my tongue, I shall give up the ghost."** So tongue on this verse pretty much means to speak, as it says; if I hold my tongue, which means, if I don't speak. So tongue does not mean evidence of salvation on this verse!

KJV-Job 15:5; **"For thy mouth uttereth thine iniquity, and thou choosest the tongue of the crafty."** So tongue on this verse means speech, as it says; and thou choosest the tongue (speech) of the crafty (devious). So tongue does not mean evidence of salvation on this verse!

KJV-Job 20:12; Though wickedness be sweet in his mouth, though he hide it under his tongue; **"Though wickedness be sweet in his mouth, though he hide it under his tongue."** So tongue on this verse actually means words, as it says; though he hide it under his tongue, which means, he hide it with his words. So tongue does not mean evidence of salvation on this verse!

KJV-Job 20:16; **"He shall suck the poison of asps: the viper's tongue shall slay him."** So tongue on this verse actually means just that, tongue, as it says; the viper's tongue shall slay him, which means the snake's (I think here viper means snake) tongue will kill him. So tongue does not mean evidence of salvation on this verse!

KJV-Job 27:4; **"My lips shall not speak wickedness, nor my tongue utter deceit."** So tongue on this verse means speech, as it says; my speech will not be deceitful. So tongue does not mean evidence of salvation on this verse!

KJV-Job 29:10; **"The nobles held their peace, and their tongue cleaved to the roof of their mouth."** So tongue on this verse means just that, tongue, as it says; and their tongue cleaved to the roof of their mouth, which is almost like saying they were tongue tied. So tongue does not mean evidence of salvation on this verse!

KJV-Job 33:2; **"Behold, now I have opened my mouth, my tongue hath spoken in my mouth."** So tongue on this verse pretty much means just that, tongue, as it says; my tongue hath spoken in my mouth, which I believe it means that he's tongue has formulated words in his mouth, or he's mumbling to himself. So tongue does not mean evidence of salvation on this verse!

KJV-Job 41:1; **"Canst thou draw out leviathan with an hook? or his tongue with a cord which thou lettest down?"** So tongue on this verse means just that, tongue, as it says; or his tongue with a chord which thou lettest down, which I'm not really sure what he's talking about, but it has something to do with using a chord and leviathan's tongue. So tongue does not mean evidence of salvation on this verse!

KJV-Psalms 5:9; **"For there is no faithfulness in their mouth; their inward part is very wickedness; their throat is an open sepulchre; they flatter with their tongue."** So tongue on this verse means speech, as it says; they flatter (sweet talk) with their tongue (speech). So tongue does not mean evidence of salvation on this verse!

KJV-Psalms 10:7; **"His mouth is full of cursing and deceit and fraud: under his tongue is mischief and vanity."** So tongue on this verse means speech, as it says; under his tongue is mischief and vanity, which means his speech is full of wickedness. So tongue does not mean evidence of salvation on this verse!

KJV-Psalms 12:3; **"The LORD shall cut off all flattering lips, and the tongue that speaketh proud things."** So tongue on this verse means just that, tongue, as it says; God will cut off the tongue that speaketh proud things. So tongue does not mean evidence of salvation on this verse!

KJV-Psalms 12:4; **"Who have said, With our tongue will we prevail; our lips are our own: who is lord over us?"** So tongue on this verse means just that, tongue, as it says; With our tongue will we prevail; our lips are our own. So tongue does not mean evidence of salvation on this verse!

KJV-Psalms 15:3; **"He that backbiteth not with his tongue, nor doeth evil to his neighbour, nor taketh up a reproach against his neighbour."** So tongue on this verse means to speak, as it says; He that backbiteth not with his tongue, which means, he who does not speak bad about somebody. So tongue does not mean evidence of salvation on this verse!

KJV-Psalms 22:15; **"My strength is dried up like a potsherd; and my tongue cleaveth to my jaws; and thou hast brought me into the dust of death."** So tongue on this verse means just that, tongue, as it says; and my tongue cleaveth to my jaws. So tongue does not mean evidence of salvation on this verse!

KJV-Psalms 31:20; **"Thou shalt hide them in the secret of thy presence from the pride of man: thou shalt keep them secretly in a pavilion from the strife of tongues."** So tongue on this verse means speech, as it says; thou shalt keep them secretly in a pavilion from the strife of tongues, which means, to keep them from harsh speech. So tongue does not mean evidence of salvation on this verse!

KJV-Psalms 34:13; **"Keep thy tongue from evil, and thy lips from speaking guile."** So tongue on this verse means just that, tongue, as it says; Keep thy tongue from evil. So tongue does not mean evidence of salvation on this verse!

KJV-Psalms 35:28; **"And my tongue shall speak of thy righteousness and of thy praise all the day long."** So tongue on this verse means speech, as it says; And my tongue shall speak of thy righteousness. So tongue does not mean evidence of salvation on this verse!

KJV-Psalms 37:30; **"The mouth of the righteous speaketh wisdom, and his tongue talketh of judgment."** So tongue on this verse means speech, as it says; and his tongue talketh of judgment. So tongue does not mean evidence of salvation on this verse!

KJV-Psalms 39:1; **(To the chief Musician, even to Jeduthun, A Psalm of David.) "I said, I will take heed to my ways, that I sin not with my tongue: I will keep my mouth with a bridle, while the wicked is before me."** So tongue on this verse means speech, as it says; that I sin not with my tongue (speech). So tongue does not mean evidence of salvation on this verse!

KJV-Psalms 39:3; **"My heart was hot within me, while I was musing the fire burned: then spake I with my tongue"** So tongue on this verse means either speech or mouth, as it says; then spake I with my tongue. So tongue does not mean evidence of salvation on this verse!

KJV-Psalms 45:1; **(To the chief Musician upon Shoshannim, for the sons of Korah, Maschil, A Song of loves.) "My heart is inditing a good matter: I speak of the things which I have made touching the king: my tongue is the pen of a ready writer."** So tongue on this verse means either speech or mouth, as it says; my tongue is the pen of a ready writer. So tongue does not mean evidence of salvation on this verse!

KJV-Psalms 50:19; **"Thou givest thy mouth to evil, and thy tongue frameth deceit."** So tongue on this verse means speech, as it says; and thy tongue frameth deceit. So tongue does not mean evidence of salvation on this verse!

KJV-Psalms 51:14; **"Deliver me from bloodguiltiness, O God, thou God of my salvation: and my tongue shall sing aloud of thy righteousness."** So tongue on this verse means either speech or mouth, as it says; and my tongue shall sing aloud of thy righteousness. So tongue does not mean evidence of salvation on this verse!

KJV-Psalms 52:2; **"Thy tongue deviseth mischiefs; like a sharp razor, working deceitfully."** So tongue on this verse means either speech or mouth, as it says; Thy tongue deviseth mischiefs. So tongue does not mean evidence of salvation on this verse!

KJV-Psalms 52:4; **"Thou lovest all devouring words, O thou deceitful tongue."** So tongue on this verse either means mouth or literally tongue itself, as it says; O thou deceitful tongue. So tongue does not mean evidence of salvation on this verse!

KJV-Psalms 55:9; **"Destroy, O Lord, and divide their tongues: for I have seen violence and strife in the city."** So tongues on this verse either means language or literally tongue itself, as it says; Destroy, O Lord, and divide their tongues. So tongue does not mean evidence of salvation on this verse!

KJV-Psalms 57:4; **"My soul is among lions: and I lie even among them that are set on fire, even the sons of men, whose teeth are spears and arrows, and their tongue a sharp sword."** So tongue on this verse means speech, as it says; and their tongue (speech) a sharp sword. So tongue does not mean evidence of salvation on this verse!

KJV-Psalms 64:3; **"Who whet their tongue like a sword, and bend their bows to shoot their arrows, even bitter words." ."** So tongue on this verse means speech, as it says; Who whet their tongue like a sword. So tongue does not mean evidence of salvation on this verse!

KJV-Psalms 64:8; **"So they shall make their own tongue to fall upon themselves: all that see them shall flee away."** So tongue on this verse means speech, as it says; So they shall make their own tongue to fall upon themselves. So tongue does not mean evidence of salvation on this verse!

KJV-Psalms 66:17; **"I cried unto him with my mouth, and he was extolled with my tongue."** So tongue on this verse means speech, as it says;

and he was extolled with my tongue. So tongue does not mean evidence of salvation on this verse!

KJV-Psalms 68:23; **"That thy foot may be dipped in the blood of thine enemies, and the tongue of thy dogs in the same."** So tongue on this verse means just that, tongue, as it says; and the tongue of thy dogs in the same. So tongue does not mean evidence of salvation on this verse!

KJV-Psalms 71:24; **"My tongue also shall talk of thy righteousness all the day long: for they are confounded, for they are brought unto shame, that seek my hurt."** So tongue on this verse means speech, as it says; My tongue also shall talk of thy righteousness all the day long. So tongue does not mean evidence of salvation on this verse!

KJV-Psalms 73:9; **"They set their mouth against the heavens, and their tongue walketh through the earth."** Wow, this is an interesting verse, isn't it!? I think this verse means; they walk around speaking badly about God and or heaven. So tongue on this verse means speech, as it says; and their tongue walketh through the earth. So tongue does not mean evidence of salvation on this verse!

KJV-Psalms 78:36; **"Nevertheless they did flatter him with their mouth, and they lied unto him with their tongues."** So tongue on this verse means speech, as it says; and they lied unto him with their tongues. So tongue does not mean evidence of salvation on this verse!

KJV-Psalms 109:2; **"For the mouth of the wicked and the mouth of the deceitful are opened against me: they have spoken against me with a lying tongue."** So tongue on this verse means speech, as it says; they have spoken against me with a lying tongue. So tongue does not mean evidence of salvation on this verse!

KJV0-Psalms 119:172; **"My tongue shall speak of thy word: for all thy commandments are righteousness."** So tongue on this verse means speech, as it says; My tongue shall speak of thy word. So tongue does not mean evidence of salvation on this verse!

KJV-Psalms 120:2; **"Deliver my soul, O LORD, from lying lips, and from a deceitful tongue."** So tongue on this verse means either speech or just tongue itself, as it says; and from a deceitful tongue. So tongue does not mean evidence of salvation on this verse!

KJV-Psalms 120:3; **"What shall be given unto thee? or what shall be done unto thee, thou false tongue?"** So tongue on this verse means either speech or just tongue itself, as it says; thou false tongue. So tongue does not mean evidence of salvation on this verse!

KJV-Psalms 126:2; **"Then was our mouth filled with laughter, and our tongue with singing: then said they among the heathen, The LORD hath done great things for them."** So tongue on this verse means either speech or just tongue itself, as it says; and our tongue with singing. So tongue does not mean evidence of salvation on this verse!

KJV-Psalms 137:6; **"If I do not remember thee, let my tongue cleave to the roof of my mouth; if I prefer not Jerusalem above my chief joy."** So tongue on this verse means just that, tongue, as it says; let my tongue cleave to the roof of my mouth, which means, let me not speak. So tongue does not mean evidence of salvation on this verse!

KJV-Psalms 139:4; **"For there is not a word in my tongue, but, lo, O LORD, thou knowest it altogether."** So tongue on this verse means just that, tongue, as it says; For there is not a word in my tongue. So tongue does not mean evidence of salvation on this verse!

KJV-Psalms 140:3; **"They have sharpened their tongues like a serpent; adders' poison is under their lips. Selah."** So tongue on this verse means just that, tongue, as it says; They have sharpened their tongues like a serpent. So tongue does not mean evidence of salvation on this verse!

KJV-Proverbs 6:17; **"A proud look, a lying tongue, and hands that shed innocent blood."** So tongue on this verse means either speech or just tongue itself, as it says; a lying tongue. So tongue does not mean evidence of salvation on this verse!

KJV-Proverbs 6:24; **"To keep thee from the evil woman, from the flattery of the tongue of a strange woman."** So tongue on this verse means either speech or voice, as it says; from the flattery of the tongue (voice) of a strange woman. So tongue does not mean evidence of salvation on this verse!

KJV-Proverbs 10:20; **"The tongue of the just is as choice silver: the heart of the wicked is little worth."** So tongue on this verse means speech, as it says; The tongue of the just is as choice silver. So tongue does not mean evidence of salvation on this verse!

KJV-Proverbs 10:31; **"The mouth of the just bringeth forth wisdom: but the froward tongue shall be cut out."** So tongue on this verse means just that, tongue, as it says; but the froward tongue shall be cut out. So tongue does not mean evidence of salvation on this verse!

KJV-Proverbs 12:18; **"There is that speaketh like the piercings of a sword: but the tongue of the wise is health."** So tongue on this verse means speech, as it says; but the tongue of the wise is health. So tongue does not mean evidence of salvation on this verse!

KJV-Proverbs 12:19; **"The lip of truth shall be established for ever: but a lying tongue is but for a moment."** So tongue on this verse means just that, tongue, as it says; but a lying tongue is but for a moment. So tongue does not mean evidence of salvation on this verse!

KJV-Proverbs 15:2; **"The tongue of the wise useth knowledge aright: but the mouth of fools poureth out foolishness."** So tongue on this verse means speech, as it says; The tongue of the wise useth knowledge aright. So tongue does not mean evidence of salvation on this verse!

KJV-Proverbs 15:4; **"A wholesome tongue is a tree of life: but perverseness therein is a breach in the spirit."** So tongue on this verse means either speech or just tongue itself, as it says; A wholesome tongue is a tree of life. So tongue does not mean evidence of salvation on this verse!

KJV-Proverbs 16:1; **"The preparations of the heart in man, and the answer of the tongue, is from the LORD."** So tongue on this verse means speech, as it says; and the answer of the tongue. So tongue does not mean evidence of salvation on this verse!

KJV-Proverbs 17:4; **"A wicked doer giveth heed to false lips; and a liar giveth ear to a naughty tongue."** So tongue on this verse means speech, as it says; and a liar giveth ear to a naughty tongue. So tongue does not mean evidence of salvation on this verse!

KJV-Proverbs 17:20; **"He that hath a froward heart findeth no good: and he that hath a perverse tongue falleth into mischief."** So tongue on this verse means speech, as it says; and he that hath a perverse tongue falleth into mischief. So tongue does not mean evidence of salvation on this verse!

KJV-Proverbs 18:21; **"Death and life are in the power of the tongue: and they that love it shall eat the fruit thereof."** So tongue on this verse means speech or words, as it says; Death and life are in the power of the tongue, which means, there's power in our words. So tongue does not mean evidence of salvation on this verse!

KJV-Proverbs 21:6; **"The getting of treasures by a lying tongue is a vanity tossed to and fro of them that seek death."** So tongue on this verse means speech, as it says; The getting of treasures by a lying tongue is a vanity, which means, lying to get stuff is no good. So tongue does not mean evidence of salvation on this verse!

KJV-Proverbs 21:23; **"Whoso keepeth his mouth and his tongue keepeth his soul from troubles."** So, this verse is very interesting, you kind of have to read between the lines, you know, you gonna have to read a few verses before it and a few verses that come right after to really understand what they were talking about to get this verse. But tongue on this verse pretty much means speech, and the verse means; whoever keeps their speech in a good manner keeps themselves from trouble. So tongue does not mean evidence of salvation on this verse!

KJV-Proverbs 25:15; **"By long forbearing is a prince persuaded, and a soft tongue breaketh the bone."** Man, Proverbs is trying to kick my butt, making me work extra hard to discern these verses, what's up with that, lol. Anyway, tongue on this verse pretty much means either speech or voice, as it says; and a soft tongue breaketh the bone, which means, a gentle speech or voice can be very powerful. So tongue does not mean evidence of salvation on this verse!

KJV-Proverbs 25:23; **"The north wind driveth away rain: so doth an angry countenance a backbiting tongue."** So tongue on this verse means speech, as it says; so doth an angry countenance a backbiting tongue, which means, a badmouthing speech. So tongue does not mean evidence of salvation on this verse!

KJV-Proverbs 26:28; **"A lying tongue hateth those that are afflicted by it; and a flattering mouth worketh ruin."** So tongue on this verse means speech, as it says; A lying tongue hateth those that are afflicted by it. So tongue does not mean evidence of salvation on this verse!

KJV-Proverbs 28:23; **"He that rebuketh a man afterwards shall find more favour than he that flattereth with the tongue."** So tongue on this verse means speech, and this verse means; a person that corrects another person who is in the wrong will find more favor (in God's eyes) than a person who just goes along so as to appease the wrong doer, you know, like a yes man. So tongue does not mean evidence of salvation on this verse!

KJV-Proverbs 31:26; **"She openeth her mouth with wisdom; and in her tongue is the law of kindness."** So tongue on this verse means speech, as it says; and in her tongue is the law of kindness, which means, she speaks very kindly. So tongue does not mean evidence of salvation on this verse!

KJV-Song of Solomon 4:11; **"Thy lips, O my spouse, drop as the honeycomb: honey and milk are under thy tongue; and the smell of thy garments is like the smell of Lebanon."** Wow, check this verse out, King Solomon getting a little romantic here, au wee wee, lol. So tongue on this verse means just that, tongue, as it says; Thy lips, O my spouse, drop as the honeycomb: honey and milk are under thy tongue, which means, her lips are looking extra sexy and delicious, lol. So tongue does not mean evidence of salvation on this verse!

KJV-Isaiah 3:8; **"For Jerusalem is ruined, and Judah is fallen: because their tongue and their doings are against the LORD, to provoke the eyes of his glory."** So tongue on this verse means speech, as it says; because their tongue and their doings are against the LORD, which means they are speaking badly about God. So tongue does not mean evidence of salvation on this verse!

KJV-Isaiah 11:15; **"And the LORD shall utterly destroy the tongue of the Egyptian sea; and with his mighty wind shall he shake his hand over the river, and shall smite it in the seven streams, and make men go over dryshod."** So tongue on this verse does not mean either speech or tongue itself, it's pretty much being used as a figure of speech, you know, to describe part of the sea like it was a tongue. And this verse is talking about the sea being parted, you know, just like how the Red sea was parted to allow the people to walk through on dry land. So tongue does not mean evidence of salvation on this verse!

KJV-Isaiah 28:11; **"For with stammering lips and another tongue will he speak to this people."** So tongue on this verse means language, and the verse is asking; will he speak to this people in a different language. So tongue does not mean evidence of salvation on this verse!

KJV-Isaiah 30:27; **"Behold, the name of the LORD cometh from far, burning with his anger, and the burden thereof is heavy: his lips are full of indignation, and his tongue as a devouring fire."** So tongue on this verse means just that, tongue, as it says; and his tongue as a devouring fire. So tongue does not mean evidence of salvation on this verse!

KJV-Isaiah 32:4; **"The heart also of the rash shall understand knowledge, and the tongue of the stammerers shall be ready to speak plainly."** So tongue on this verse means speech, as it says; and the tongue of the stammerers shall be ready to speak plainly. So tongue does not mean evidence of salvation on this verse!

KJV-Isaiah 33:19; **"Thou shalt not see a fierce people, a people of a deeper speech than thou canst perceive; of a stammering tongue, that thou canst not understand."** So tongue on this verse means language, as it says; of a stammering tongue, that thou canst not understand. So tongue does not mean evidence of salvation on this verse!

KJV-Isaiah 35:6; **"Then shall the lame man leap as an hart, and the tongue of the dumb sing: for in the wilderness shall waters break out, and streams in the desert."** So tongue on this verse means just that, tongue, as it says; and the tongue of the dumb sing. So tongue does not mean evidence of salvation on this verse!

KJV-Isaiah 41:17; **"When the poor and needy seek water, and there is none, and their tongue faileth for thirst, I the LORD will hear them, I the God of Israel will not forsake them."** So tongue on this verse means just that, tongue, as it says; and their tongue faileth for thirst. So tongue does not mean evidence of salvation on this verse!

KJV-Isaiah 45:23; **"I have sworn by myself, the word is gone out of my mouth in righteousness, and shall not return, That unto me every knee shall bow, every tongue shall swear."** So tongue on this verse does not mean either speech or tongue itself, it's pretty much being used as a figure of speech, you know, like saying everybody will swear. So tongue does not mean evidence of salvation on this verse!

KJV-Isaiah 50:4; **"The Lord GOD hath given me the tongue of the learned, that I should know how to speak a word in season to him that is weary: he wakeneth morning by morning, he wakeneth mine ear to hear as the learned."** So tongue on this verse means speech, as it says; The Lord GOD hath given me the tongue (speech) of the learned, that I should know how to speak a word in season to him that is weary, which means, God has given him the ability to speak wisely. So tongue does not mean evidence of salvation on this verse!

KJV-Isaiah 54:17; **"No weapon that is formed against thee shall prosper; and every tongue that shall rise against thee in judgment thou shalt condemn. This is the heritage of the servants of the LORD, and their righteousness is of me, saith the LORD."** So tongue on this verse does not mean either speech or tongue itself, it's pretty much being used as a figure of speech, you know, like saying; if anybody shall rise against thee. So tongue does not mean evidence of salvation on this verse!

KJV-Isaiah 57:4: **"Against whom do ye sport yourselves? against whom make ye a wide mouth, and draw out the tongue? are ye not children of transgression, a seed of falsehood."** So tongue on this verse means speech, as it says; against whom make ye a wide mouth, and draw out the tongue, which I believe means, who are you to speak boldly. So tongue does not mean evidence of salvation on this verse!

KJV-Isaiah 59:3; **"For your hands are defiled with blood, and your fingers with iniquity; your lips have spoken lies, your tongue hath** muttered perverseness." So tongue on this verse means speech, as it says; your tongue hath muttered perverseness. So tongue does not mean evidence of salvation on this verse!

KJV-Isaiah 66:18; **"For I know their works and their thoughts: it shall come, that I will gather all nations and tongues; and they shall come, and see my glory."** So tongues on this verse means languages, as it says; that I will gather all nations and tongues. So tongues does not mean evidence of salvation on this verse!

KJV-Jeremiah 9:3; **"And they bend their tongues like their bow for lies: but they are not valiant for the truth upon the earth; for they proceed from evil to evil, and they know not me, saith the LORD."** So tongues on this verse means just that, tongues, as it says; And they bend their tongues like their bow for lies. So tongues does not mean evidence of salvation on this verse!

KJV-Jeremiah 9:5; **"And they will deceive every one his neighbour, and will not speak the truth: they have taught their tongue to speak lies, and weary themselves to commit iniquity."** So tongue on this verse means either mouth or just that, tongue, as it says; they have taught their tongue to speak lies. So tongue does not mean evidence of salvation on this verse!

KJV-Jeremiah 9:8; **"Their tongue is as an arrow shot out; it speaketh deceit: one speaketh peaceably to his neighbour with his mouth, but in heart he layeth his wait."** So tongue on this verse means speech, as it says; Their tongue is as an arrow shot out; it speaketh deceit. So tongue does not mean evidence of salvation on this verse!

KJV-Jeremiah 18:18; **"Then said they, Come, and let us devise devices against Jeremiah; for the law shall not perish from the priest, nor counsel from the wise, nor the word from the prophet. Come, and let us smite him with the tongue, and let us not give heed to any of his** words." So tongue on this verse means speech, as it says; and let us smite him with the tongue, which means, let's talk badly about him. So tongue does not mean evidence of salvation on this verse!

KJV-Jeremiah 23:31; **"Behold, I am against the prophets, saith the LORD, that use their tongues, and say, He saith."** So tongue on this verse means speech, as it says; that use their tongues, and say, He saith. So tongue does not mean evidence of salvation on this verse!

KJV-Lamentations 4:4; **"The tongue of the sucking child cleaveth to the roof of his mouth for thirst: the young children ask bread, and no man breaketh it unto them."** So tongue on this verse means just that, tongue, as it says; The tongue of the sucking child cleaveth to the roof of his mouth for thirst. So tongue does not mean evidence of salvation on this verse!

KJV-Ezekiel 3:26; **"And I will make thy tongue cleave to the roof of thy mouth, that thou shalt be dumb, and shalt not be to them a reprover: for they are a rebellious house."** So tongue on this verse means just that, tongue, as it says; And I will make thy tongue cleave to the roof of thy mouth, that thou shalt be dumb, which means, they will be made not able to speak. So tongue does not mean evidence of salvation on this verse!

KJV-Daniel 1:4; **"Children in whom was no blemish, but well favoured, and skilful in all wisdom, and cunning in knowledge, and understanding science, and such as had ability in them to stand in the king's palace, and whom they might teach the learning and the tongue of the Chaldeans."** So tongue on this verse means language, as it says; and whom they might teach the learning and the tongue of the Chaldeans. So tongue does not mean evidence of salvation on this verse!

KJV-Hosea 7:16; **"They return, but not to the most High: they are like a deceitful bow: their princes shall fall by the sword for the rage of their tongue: this shall be their derision in the land of Egypt." So tongue on this verse means speech, as it says; their princes shall fall by the sword for the rage of their tongue. So tongue does not mean evidence of salvation on this verse!

KJV-Amos 6:10; **"And a man's uncle shall take him up, and he that burneth him, to bring out the bones out of the house, and shall say unto him that is by the sides of the house, Is there yet any with thee? and he shall say, No. Then shall he say, Hold thy tongue: for we may not make mention of the name of the LORD."** So tongue on this verse means speech, as it says; Then shall he say, Hold thy tongue, which means, hold up, don't speak. So tongue does not mean evidence of salvation on this verse!

KJV-Micah 6:12; **"For the rich men thereof are full of violence, and the inhabitants thereof have spoken lies, and their tongue is deceitful in their mouth."** So tongue on this verse means speech, as it says; and the inhabitants thereof have spoken lies, and their tongue is deceitful in their mouth. So tongue does not mean evidence of salvation on this verse!

KJV-Habakkuk 1:13; **"Thou art of purer eyes than to behold evil, and canst not look on iniquity: wherefore lookest thou upon them that deal treacherously, and holdest thy tongue when the wicked devoureth the man that is more righteous than he?"** So tongue on this verse means speech, as it says; and holdest thy tongue, which means, and doesn't say anything. So tongue does not mean evidence of salvation on this verse!

KJV-Zephaniah 3:13; **"The remnant of Israel shall not do iniquity, nor speak lies; neither shall a deceitful tongue be found in their mouth: for they shall feed and lie down, and none shall make them afraid."** So tongue on this verse means speech, as it says; neither shall a deceitful tongue be found in their mouth. So tongue does not mean evidence of salvation on this verse!

KJV-Zechariah 14:12; **"And this shall be the plague wherewith the LORD will smite all the people that have fought against Jerusalem; Their flesh shall consume away while they stand upon their feet, and their eyes shall consume away in their holes, and their tongue shall consume away in their mouth."** So tongue on this verse means just that, tongue, as it says; and their tongue shall consume away in their mouth. So tongue does not mean evidence of salvation on this verse!

KJV-Mark 7:33; **"And he took him aside from the multitude, and put his fingers into his ears, and he spit, and touched his tongue."** So tongue on this verse means just that, tongue, as it says; and touched his tongue. So tongue does not mean evidence of salvation on this verse!

KJV-Mark 7:35; **"And straightway his ears were opened, and the string of his tongue was loosed, and he spake plain."** So tongue on this verse means just that, tongue, as it says; and the string of his tongue was loosed, and he spake plain. So tongue does not mean evidence of salvation on this verse!

KJV-Mark 16:17; **"And these signs shall follow them that believe; In my name shall they cast out devils; they shall speak with new tongues."** So tongues on this verse means languages, as it says; they shall speak with new tongues, which means they will speak in different languages. Now, I think this is one of the verses that people who believe in the "speaking in tongues" doctrine use to justify their doctrine. And so what I wanna do now, I want us to double check this verse, and we gonna do this checking out a few verses that come before and a few verses that come after this verse so as to get the full content of the meaning of this verse. So here we go, let's double check this verse out!

<u>14</u> "Afterward he appeared unto the eleven as they sat at meat, and upbraided them with their unbelief and hardness of heart, because they believed not them which had seen him after he was risen. <u>15</u> And he said unto them, Go ye into all the world, and preach the gospel to every creature. <u>16</u> He

that believeth and is baptized shall be saved; but he that believeth not shall be damned. **17 And these signs shall follow them that believe; In my name shall they cast out devils; they shall speak with new tongues;** 18 They shall take up serpents; and if they drink any deadly thing, it shall not hurt them; they shall lay hands on the sick, and they shall recover. 19 So then after the Lord had spoken unto them, he was received up into heaven, and sat on the right hand of God. 20 And they went forth, and preached every where, the Lord working with *them*, and confirming the word with signs following. Amen."

So, what do you think, after reading the verses before and the verses that come after verse **17** (the verse we double checking on), what does speaking in tongues mean to you now!? Does it mean evidence of salvation or does it mean languages? To me, speaking in tongues on this verse still refers to speaking in different languages. And the reason I came to this conclusion is because, you see how it says; (verse 15) "And he said unto them, Go ye into all the world, and preach the gospel to every creature," well, in order for them to really be effective in preaching the gospel all over the world, they would greatly benefit from knowing how to speak the different languages that people speak all over the world, you know what I mean? And so this is why Jesus gave them the ability to speak in new tongues (languages), you know, so they can easily preach the gospel in the language of whatever country and or nation they travelled to. And also, they were also given the ability to cast out demons and to also be able to heal the sick, which went hand in hand with their ability to speak in tongues. And all this was for the benefit of spreading the gospel, as they worked miracles of healing the sick and casting out demons, which was a sign that a believer was given by Jesus to serve as a witness of the power of God in Jesus Christ.

Ok, so, what do you think now about "speaking in tongues", is it a language or evidence of salvation!? To me, it makes a lot of sense with it meaning language than it meaning evidence of salvation, because if you think about it, if it meant evidence of salvation, not only would Jesus most likely plainly say so, but we would up to this day be able to cast out demons and heal the sick just like they did back then, you know, because those powers came along with speaking in tongues. And to make it absolutely clear, when I say cast out demons and heal the sick I'm not talking about praying for healing today and waiting a few weeks and or months for the healing to happen, oh no, nope, I'm talking about immediate healing and casting out of demons just like how it used to happen back then, you know, because that's how Jesus worked, you know, His miracles were immediate, you know what I mean? Anyway, if you still are not convinced that speaking in tongues actually means speaking in different languages, ok, let's check out some more verses and see what they have to say about it!

KJV-Luke 1:64; **"And his mouth was opened immediately, and his tongue loosed, and he spake, and praised God."** So tongue on this verse means just that, tongue, as it says; and his tongue loosed, and he spake, and praised God. So tongue does not mean evidence of salvation on this verse!

KJV-Luke 16:24; **"And he cried and said, Father Abraham, have mercy on me, and send Lazarus, that he may dip the tip of his finger in water, and cool my tongue; for I am tormented in this flame."** So tongue on this verse means just that, tongue, as it says; and cool my tongue; for I am tormented in this flame. So tongue does not mean evidence of salvation on this verse!

KJV-John 5:2; **"Now there is at Jerusalem by the sheep market a pool, which is called in the Hebrew tongue Bethesda, having five porches."** So tongue on this verse means language, as it says; which is called in the Hebrew tongue Bethesda. So tongue does not mean evidence of salvation on this verse!

KJV-Acts 1:19; **"And it was known unto all the dwellers at Jerusalem; insomuch as that field is called in their proper tongue, Aceldama, that is to say, The field of blood."** So tongue on this verse means language, as it says; insomuch as that field is called in their proper tongue, Aceldama, that is to say, The field of blood. So tongue does not mean evidence of salvation on this verse!

KJV-Acts 2:3; **"And there appeared unto them cloven tongues like as of fire, and it sat upon each of them."** So tongues on this verse means languages, as it says; And there appeared unto them cloven tongues like as of fire, which means, several languages that looked like fire appeared into them. So tongues does not mean evidence of salvation on this verse!

KJV-Acts 2:4; **"And they were all filled with the Holy Ghost, and began to speak with other tongues, as the Spirit gave them utterance."** So tongues on this verse means languages, as it says; and began to speak with other tongues, as the Spirit gave them utterance, which means, they began to speak in other languages as the Spirit gave them the ability to speak in those languages. Now, I think this is probably the main verse that people who believe in speaking in tongues use to justify their doctrine, so let's go ahead and double check it again by examining the full context of what this verse is talking about. And of course we gonna do this double checking by examining the few verses that come before and after this verse so as to get the full context of the meaning of this verse. Ok, so here we go!

1 "And when the day of Pentecost was fully come, they were all with one accord in one place. 2 And suddenly there came a sound from heaven as of a rushing mighty wind, and it filled all the house where they were sitting. 3 And there appeared unto them cloven tongues like as of fire, and it sat upon each of them. **4 And they were all filled with the Holy Ghost, and began to speak with other tongues, as the Spirit gave them utterance.** 5 And there were dwelling at Jerusalem Jews, devout men, out of every nation under heaven. 6 Now when this was noised abroad, the multitude came together, and were confounded, because that every man heard them speak in his own language. 7 And they were all amazed and marvelled, saying one to another, Behold, are not all these which speak

Galilaeans?" Ok, so what do you think, did you get it, did you understand the full context, or do you need me to explain it. Ok fine, since you insist, I'll explain it, not a problem, that's what I'm here for, lol

Ok, so, anyway, what's really going on here is that; it's the day of Pentecost and the disciples are all together sitting in a house and all of a sudden they heard a mighty wind and then they saw cloven tongues (languages) that looked like fire (and the fire represents the power of God) all on top of each one of them, and then God filled them with the Holy Ghost and they began to speak in different languages as the Holy Ghost gave them the ability to speak those languages. Now, you wanna know how we can be extra sure that tongues on this verse means languages (languages that people can understand), check out verse 6, you see how it says; **"Now when this was noised abroad, the multitude came together, and were confounded, because that every man heard them speak in his own language,"** did you see that, it said; **"every man heard them speak in his own language,"** wow, the people actually heard the disciples speaking clearly in each person's native language, you know, the people could understand exactly what the disciples were saying, even though the people were all from different nations and spoke different languages.

So, it's very clear that the speaking in tongues here definitely means speaking in different languages as the Spirit gave them utterance when they got filled with the Holy Ghost. And so, if we apply this meaning to our time today, it would mean that the people who believe in speaking in tongues (as they practice it) would have to speak in a clear language that everyone in attendance can understand what they are saying, you know, just like how the people understood what the disciples where saying as the Spirit gave them utterance, you know what I mean? And so, these verses right here pretty much disqualifies and or does not justify the doctrine of speaking in tongues as it is practiced by the people who believe in it, you know, instead of speaking in a clear language as the Spirit gives them utterance, they instead speak in gibberish, you know, they speak in a strange language (which is not even a language) which no one can understand. And so, these verses right here are not favorable to the people that believe in speaking in tongues, let's check out some more verses that deal with tongues and see what they have to say about it!

KJV-Acts 2:8; **"And how hear we every man in our own tongue, wherein we were born?"** So tongue on this verse means language, and the verse asks; how is it that we are able to hear them in our own (each person's) language from where we were born. So tongue does not mean evidence of salvation on this verse!

KJV-Acts 2:11; **"Cretes and Arabians, we do hear them speak in our tongues the wonderful works of God."** So tongues on this verse means languages, as it says; Cretes and Arabians (two different nations), we do hear them speak in our languages the wonderful works of God. Now, let me ask you, when the people practice speaking in tongues nowadays do speak it, do the people in attendance hear and or understand what they are saying about the wonderful works of God? And the answer of course is a big fat NO, so that right there has got to tell you that something is wrong with the doctrine and it should be double checked to make sure it is sound, because from this verse the doctrine is not sound at all, am I right or wrong? Let's check out some more verses on tongues!

KJV-Acts 2:26; **"Therefore did my heart rejoice, and my tongue was glad; moreover also my flesh shall rest in hope."** So tongue on this verse means either speech or just that, tongue, as it says; and my tongue was glad. So tongue does not mean evidence of salvation on this verse!

KJV-Acts 10:46; **"For they heard them speak with tongues, and magnify God. Then answered Peter."** Let's check out this verse in its full context, because I think this is another verse that people who believe in speaking in tongues use to justify their doctrine.

43 "To him give all the prophets witness, that through his name whosoever believeth in him shall receive remission of sins. 44 While Peter yet spake these words, the Holy Ghost fell on all them which heard the word.

<u>45</u> And they of the circumcision which believed were astonished, as many as came with Peter, because that on the Gentiles also was poured out the gift of the Holy Ghost. **<u>46</u> For they heard them speak with tongues, and magnify God. Then answered Peter,** <u>47</u> Can any man forbid water, that these should not be baptized, which have received the Holy Ghost as well as we? <u>48</u> And he commanded them to be baptized in the name of the Lord. Then prayed they him to tarry certain days."

Ok, so let me summarize what's happening on these verses. And what's happening is; Peter was telling the people that if they believe in Jesus Christ their sins will be forgiven and they will receive salvation, and as he was speaking, the Holy Ghost fell on all the people that believed (Jews and Gentiles) and they all received the gift of tongues and started praising God in different languages. You know what, I think this is actually the main verse that got the people who believe in speaking in tongues confused at it's meaning, which led them to (and still leads them) to misinterpret what speaking in tongues really means. And this is why it is very important to compare scripture with other scriptures that talk about the same topic, you know, so you can really examine and see if there is another scripture that might re-explain and or contradict what you thought the verse you was trying to discern really means. But so anyway, yeah, tongues on this verse (46) means languages, and we can be sure of that by the fact that the people heard them magnify God, which means the people spoke in actual languages that can be understood, because if they didn't, people would be trying to figure out what they were saying, you know, and a question like; what manner of speech is this, would probably have followed as the people spoke in tongues. And I can see Peter telling them something like; for they speak in a spiritual language that only them and God can understand, for this is the evidence of their salvation. I mean, what do you think, wouldn't this be a great occasion for Peter to tell them that. But, of course Peter did not tell them that, and that is because the gift of tongues is only one in many other gifts that the Holy Ghost gives to those who believe in Jesus Christ. Let's check out some more verses!

KJV-Acts 19:6; "**And when Paul had laid his hands upon them, the Holy Ghost came on them; and they spake with tongues, and prophesied."** Let's check out the full context of this verse, because it's pretty powerful!

<u>3</u> "And he said unto them, Unto what then were ye baptized? And they said, Unto John's baptism. <u>4</u> Then said Paul, John verily baptized with the baptism of repentance, saying unto the people, that they should believe on him which should come after him, that is, on Christ Jesus. <u>5</u> When they heard *this*, they were baptized in the name of the Lord Jesus. <u>6</u> **And when Paul had laid *his* hands upon them, the Holy Ghost came on them; and they spake with tongues, and prophesied."** So, what I really wanted you to see on these verses here is how immediately the Holy Ghost comes to a person who believes in Christ. And the reason why I wanted you see that is because, the way the people who believe in speaking in tongues teach about the Holy Ghost is that, you not really saved until you speak in tongues, but since speaking in tongues can only happen when you receive the Holy Ghost, that means that the day you repent of your sins and accept Jesus Christ as your Lord and Savior is not the day you actually get saved and receive the Holy Ghost, you know, because you don't yet speak in tongues, which they say is the evidence of having received the Holy Ghost, which means you are now saved.

So if you believe in this theology, that would mean that, even though you repented of your sins and accepted Jesus Christ as your Lord and Savior and you got baptized today, that doesn't mean you will receive the Holy Ghost today, oh no, that means you still got some more work to do to receive the Holy Ghost, which will finally mean that you are saved. I mean, are you following what I'm saying here, are you catching my drift, I surely hope so, because this is a very important topic (salvation), which has grossly been misinterpreted by the speaking in tongues believers. And you don't have to take my words for it, you know, to believe that it's a totally false interpretation, I mean, you can just check out verses 5 and 6 above, which says; <u>5</u> **"When they heard *this*, they were baptized in the** name of the Lord Jesus. **6 And when Paul had laid *his* hands upon them, the Holy Ghost came on them; and they spake with tongues, and prophesied."** Ok, so, you see, as soon as the people got baptized and Paul laid his hands on them the Holy Ghost right away came on them and they right away started speaking in tongues. So what does that tell you, it tells me that the Holy Ghost comes into a person as soon as the person repent of their sins and believes in Jesus Christ as their Lord and Savior, you know, which means the person doesn't have to seek out the Holy Ghost after they have already accepted Jesus Christ as their Lord and Savior, I mean, that action of the Holy Ghost entering the person is an immediate action, as it is shown by the two verses above. And so Salvation is an immediate action, one that is given to us freely, and it happens as soon as we repent of our sins and accept Jesus Christ as our Lord and Savior, that's it, we don't need to go seeking after anything else, Christ puts the Holy Ghost in us as soon as we accept Him. And as far as speaking in tongues, not everyone receives that gift of the Holy Ghost, there's many more gifts of the Holy Ghost, speaking in tongues is just one of them, as we'll see as we check out some more verses that talk about tongues.

KJV-Acts 21:40; **"And when he had given him licence, Paul stood on the stairs, and beckoned with the hand unto the people. And when there was made a great silence, he spake unto them in the Hebrew tongue, saying"** So tongue on this verse means language, as it says; he spake unto them in the Hebrew tongue, saying. So tongue does not mean evidence of salvation on this verse!

KJV-Acts 22:2; **"And when they heard that he spake in the Hebrew tongue to them, they kept the more silence: and he saith."** So tongue on this verse means language, as it says; And when they heard that he spake in the Hebrew tongue to them. So tongue does not mean evidence of salvation on this verse!

KJV-Acts 26:14; **"And when we were all fallen to the earth, I heard a voice speaking unto me, and saying in the Hebrew tongue, Saul,**

Saul, why persecutest thou me? it is hard for thee to kick against the pricks." So tongue on this verse means language, as it says; I heard a voice speaking unto me, and saying in the Hebrew tongue. So tongue does not mean evidence of salvation on this verse!

KJV-Romans 3:13; **"Their throat is an open sepulchre; with their tongues they have used deceit; the poison of asps is under their lips"** So tongues on this verse means speech, as it says; with their tongues they have used deceit, which means, they used their speech to deceive. So tongues does not mean evidence of salvation on this verse!

KJV-Romans 14:11; **"For it is written, As I live, saith the Lord, every knee shall bow to me, and every tongue shall confess to God."** So tongue on this verse means either speech or just that, tongue, as it says; and every tongue shall confess to God. So tongue does not mean evidence of salvation on this verse!

KJV-1 Corinthians 12:10; **"To another the working of miracles; to another prophecy; to another discerning of spirits; to another divers kinds of tongues; to another the interpretation of tongues."** Ok, let's check out the full context of this verse, because this verse is actually probably one of the most powerful verses that discredit the speaking in tongues doctrine.

7 "But the manifestation of the Spirit is given to every man to profit withal. 8 For to one is given by the Spirit the word of wisdom; to another the word of knowledge by the same Spirit; 9 To another faith by the same Spirit; to another the gifts of healing by the same Spirit; **10 To another the working of miracles; to another prophecy; to another discerning of spirits; to another *divers* kinds of tongues; to another the interpretation of tongues:** 11 But all these worketh that one and the selfsame Spirit, dividing to every man severally as he will. 12 For as the body is one, and hath many members, and all the members of that one body, being many, are one body: so also *is* Christ. 13 For by one Spirit are we all baptized into

one body, whether *we be* Jews or Gentiles, whether *we be* bond or free; and have been all made to drink into one Spirit."

Ok, so, let's start with verse 7, and what verse 7 means is that, every man is given the gift of the Spirit to profit with, which means, to make good use of. And then verse 8, which says that each person receives a different kind of gift of the Spirit, you know, some receive the gift of wisdom, some receive the gift of healing, some receive the gift of prophecy, some receive the gift of tongues, and so on. And so what this verse tells us is that, not everybody receives all the gifts of the Holy Ghost, you know, everybody receives whatever gifts the Holy Ghost wants to give to that person, you know, as verse 11 says; **But all these worketh that one and the selfsame Spirit, dividing to every man severally as he will.** So what this verse tells us is that, not everyone will receive the gift of tongues, which means not everyone will be able to speak in tongues, you know, which will mean that there's no way speaking in tongues can be the evidence of a person's salvation, because if it was, they everyone saved would have to receive it, you know what I mean? I mean it's crazy, but I wonder how many people who believe in the speaking in tongues doctrine have really taken the time to look and or examine this verse, because truth be told, these verses right here are not even that hard to discern at all, I mean, they are pretty much straight forward, you know, a person doesn't really have to be a student of theology to understand these verses right here, you know what I mean? I mean it's crazy, I really having a hard time understanding how anybody can misinterpret these verses right here, you know, **1 Corinthians 12:10** could not have been written as simple as it was, you know what I mean? So come on people give me a break, this is a very powerful verse, it totally discredits speaking in tongues as being evidence of a person's salvation. I mean, I don't know what else to say on this, but you know what, ok, let's check out some more verses that talk about speaking in tongues and see what they have to say about it!

KJV-1 Corinthians 12:28; **"And God hath set some in the church, first apostles, secondarily prophets, thirdly teachers, after that miracles,**

then gifts of healings, helps, governments, diversities of tongues." So tongues on this verse means languages, as it says; diversities of tongues, which means, different kinds of tongues, which means, different kinds of languages. So tongues does not mean evidence of salvation on this verse!

KJV-1 Corinthians 12:30; **"Have all the gifts of healing? do all speak with tongues? do all interpret?"** So tongues on this verse means languages, as it says; do all speak with tongues? So on this verse (I believe this was Apostle Paul speaking), Paul is reminding them that not all will have the same gifts, and he does this by asking them sarcastically about the gifts. I mean, it's almost like asking (for example), is everyone gifted to play basketball, is everyone gifted to play football, is everyone gifted to play baseball, and of course the answer is no, not everyone is gifted to play all three of these sports, you know, some are gifted in basketball, some are gifted in football, and some are gifted in baseball. And so using this analogy, when Paul asks; **do all speak with tongues?** He's not asking do all of them speak in tongues yet (which is what the people who practice speaking in tongues think that is what Paul is asking), no, not at all, Paul is actually telling them that not all will have the gift of tongues. Did you get it, did you understand it? I hope you did, because this verse is a little bit tricky, but I think I gave a pretty good analogy with the sports thing, what you think, can I pat myself on the back for this one or not, lol So tongues does not mean evidence of salvation on this verse!

KJV-1 Corinthians 13:1; **"Though I speak with the tongues of men and of angels, and have not charity, I am become as sounding brass, or a tinkling cymbal."** So tongues on this verse means languages, as it says; Though I speak with the tongues of men and of angels. Now, did you notice how Paul said that, even though he speaks with the tongues of men and of angels, if he does not have kindness (**charity**), he is nothing (**I am become as sounding brass, or a tinkling cymbal**). So what Paul is implying here is that, speaking in tongues has no value if you don't have kindness in your heart. So tongues does not mean evidence of salvation on this verse!

KJV-1 Corinthians 13:8; **"Charity never faileth: but whether there be prophecies, they shall fail; whether there be tongues, they shall cease; whether there be knowledge, it shall vanish away."** So tongues on this verse means languages, as it says; whether there be tongues, they shall cease, which means, tongues can stop. So tongues does not mean evidence of salvation on this verse!

KJV-1 Corinthians 14:2; **"For he that speaketh in an unknown tongue speaketh not unto men, but unto God: for no man understandeth him; howbeit in the spirit he speaketh mysteries."** Alright, I think this is actually the main verse that people who believe in speaking in tongues use to justify their doctrine, so let's check out the full context of this verse and see what it is really saying!

<u>1</u> "Follow after charity, and desire spiritual *gifts*, but rather that ye may prophesy. <u>2</u> **For he that speaketh in an *unknown* tongue speaketh not unto men, but unto God: for no man understandeth *him*; howbeit in the spirit he speaketh mysteries.** <u>3</u> But he that prophesieth speaketh unto men *to* edification, and exhortation, and comfort. <u>4</u> He that speaketh in an *unknown* tongue edifieth himself; but he that prophesieth edifieth the church. <u>5</u> I would that ye all spake with tongues, but rather that ye prophesied: for greater *is* he that prophesieth than he that speaketh with tongues, except he interpret, that the church may receive edifying."

Ok, so, notice how the first verse says; **"Follow after charity, and desire spiritual *gifts*, but rather that ye may prophesy,"** and what Apostle Paul is saying here is that, it's ok to desire spiritual gifts, but it would be better if we could prophesy (which means to have the ability to know of things to come, it's like to have revelations of things to come, both in this life and in after life). Then we get to the second verse (the verse we are working on), which says; **"For he that speaketh in an *unknown* tongue speaketh not unto men, but unto God: for no man understandeth *him*; howbeit in the spirit he speaketh mysteries."** And what this verse is saying is that, a person that speaks in an unknown language is not speaking to men, but to God, which means, only God can understand what the person is saying, you know, because God understands all languages, am I right or wrong? And then, you see how it says; **"howbeit in the spirit he speaketh mysteries,"** and what this means is, since no one can understand what the speaker is saying, whatever the spear is saying pretty much becomes mysterious, you know, unknown, because no one can understand what he is saying. And so this verse does not mean that whatever the speaker is saying is an unknown spiritual language that is a direct secret personal communication between human beings and God, that even the devil can't understand (as the people who believe in speaking in tongues claim it to be), but that is false, that is a misinterpretation of this verse. And, if we can just be real for a second here, why would God want to have a secret language with us when He can pretty much already read our minds and know what we are thinking about even before we ourselves come to full recognition of what we are thinking. So come on man, give me a break, let's stop with all this elementary reasoning already, this is not hard stuff to discern. And also, why would God want the devil not to be able to understand what we are talking to God about, because truth be told, most of our conversation with God involves us either thanking Him, or praising Him, or worshipping Him, and so why would God not want the devil to hear us thanking, praising and or worshipping Him, I mean, does that make any sense to you, to me it doesn't?!

So once again I say, come on man, give me a break, let's stop making up stuff that don't make any sense, you know, we are all grown folks here (I'm supposing that mostly grown folks will be reading this book), so let's start acting like it, and let's start correcting all these misinterpretations, because that is what the Bible calls for us to do, and as grown folks, we should not be afraid to do so, that way we can teach our children sound doctrines, so they don't grow up to be ignorant adults, as we are showing ourselves to be, by continuing to believe in false doctrines. But I refuse to be an ignorant adult, and I refuse to let you be an ignorant adult either, so let's continue to check out some more verses about tongues and see what they have to say!

KJV-1 Corinthians 14:4; **"He that speaketh in an unknown tongue edifieth himself; but he that prophesieth edifieth the church."** So tongue on this verse means language, as it says; He that speaketh in an unknown tongue edifieth himself. Now, did you notice how it says that a person who speaks in unknown tongue (language) edifieth (enlightens) himself, but a person who prophesieth (teaches) enlightens the church. And so what this means is that, it's better to prophesy than to speak in unknown tongue (which is what the people who practice speaking in tongues do, you know, they speak in an unknown tongue, and I mean actually, they don't even speak in a tongue at all, they speak in an unknown gibberish, you know what I mean? And so tongue on this verse definitely does not mean evidence of salvation!

KJV-1 Corinthians 14:5; **"I would that ye all spake with tongues, but rather that ye prophesied: for greater is he that prophesieth than he that speaketh with tongues, except he interpret, that the church may receive edifying."** Wow, I wonder how many people who believe in speaking in tongues have really read this verse, because this verse is actually saying that a person who speaks in tongues is lower (in the spiritual gifts category) than a person that prophesies. I mean, wow, did you catch that!? Also, did you catch how it says; **except he interpret, that the church may receive edifying.** Well, I got a question for you, how often have you heard anybody interpreting what they are saying when they speak in tongues? Well, the answer is pretty much almost never, no not almost, the answer is actually never, am I right or wrong? I mean have you ever heard anybody interpreting what the person is saying when they are speaking in tongues (as the believers of it practice it nowadays), you most likely haven't, and I for sure have never have. And so tongues on this verse definitely does not mean evidence of salvation, because if it did, it by no means would be a lesser gift of the Holy Spirit, no way, no no no no, nope, no way!

KJV-1 Corinthians 14:6; **"Now, brethren, if I come unto you speaking with tongues, what shall I profit you, except I shall speak to**

you either by revelation, or by knowledge, or by prophesying, or by doctrine?" So tongues on this verse means languages, as it says; Now, brethren, if I come unto you speaking with tongues, what shall I profit you, which means, if I come to you speaking in different languages what good am I to you, because you won't be able to understand what I'm saying. So tongues does not mean evidence of salvation on this verse!

KJV-1 Corinthians 14:9; **"So likewise ye, except ye utter by the tongue words easy to be understood, how shall it be known what is spoken? for ye shall speak into the air."** Oh wow, this verse right here, this verse right here, did you understand what this verse just said!? This verse just said that when you speak in tongue you should say words that are easy to be understood, otherwise no one will understand you, and therefore it will be like you are just speaking into the air. Wow, wow, wow, did you get it, did you understand it, I mean, this verse just described exactly what the people who practice speaking in tongues do, you know, they use words that no one can understand, and therefore they are pretty much speaking into the air, which means, whatever they are saying doesn't benefit anybody, which is what speaking in tongues supposed to do, you know, benefit the people around them, you know, edify the church. And so this verse totally discredits the speaking in tongues doctrine, it renders it totally useless, from how it is being practiced nowadays, I mean, am I right or wrong? And so tongue on this verse definitely does not mean evidence of salvation!

KJV-1 Corinthians 14:13; **"Wherefore let him that speaketh in an unknown tongue pray that he may interpret."** So tongue on this verse means language, and what this verse means is; hopefully the person who speaks in an unknown tongue will have the ability to interpret it. And so tongue on this verse does not mean evidence of salvation!

KJV-1 Corinthians 14:14; **"For if I pray in an unknown tongue, my spirit prayeth, but my understanding is unfruitful."** So tongue on this verse means language, and what this verse means is; if you pray in an unknown language, even though your spirit gives you utterance, you get no benefit from it, because you don't understand what you yourself are saying. And so tongue on this verse does not mean evidence of salvation!

KJV-1 Corinthians 14:18; **"I thank my God, I speak with tongues more than ye all."** So tongues on this verse means languages, and what this verse means is; He thanks God that he speaks in more languages than the rest of them. Now, I think the people who believe in speaking in tongues think this verse is saying that He thanks God that he speaks in tongues a lot more than the rest of them, but no, that's not what it means, it means He speaks in more languages than the rest of them. And so tongues on this verse does not mean evidence of salvation!

KJV-1 Corinthians 14:19; **"Yet in the church I had rather speak five words with my understanding, that by my voice I might teach others also, than ten thousand words in an unknown tongue."** So tongue on this verse means language, and what this verse means is; He would rather speak five words in a language he understands than speak ten thousand words in a language he doesn't understand. And so tongue on this verse does not mean evidence of salvation!

KJV-1 Corinthians 14:21; **"In the law it is written, With men of other tongues and other lips will I speak unto this people; and yet for all that will they not hear me, saith the Lord."** So tongues on this verse means languages, as it says; With men of other tongues and other lips will I speak unto this people. And so tongues on this verse does not mean evidence of salvation!

KJV-1 Corinthians 14:22; **"Wherefore tongues are for a sign, not to them that believe, but to them that believe not: but prophesying serveth not for them that believe not, but for them which believe."** Oh man, wow, this verse here, I think this verse just put the nail to the coffin of the speaking in tongues doctrine. I mean, wow, oh man, oh boy, oh my Lord, help us please, have mercy on us, for we don't mean to purposely misinterpret scriptures, it's just that a lot of us are blinded, our spiritual eyes and our spiritual ears are closed, so we have a hard time seeing the true meaning of the verses, and our ears have a hard time hearing truth when it's told to us, so we ask you in Jesus name to please open our spiritual eyes and our spiritual ears so we can easily understand the verses so we can correct our errors, because we really want to thank, praise and worship you in truth and with a pure heart, thank you Lord, thank you Lord, in Jesus's name we pray, Amen!

Ok, I had to say a little prayer before I went over this verse with you, because this verse is very powerful, this verse pretty much contradicts the doctrine of speaking in tongues, this verse pretty much really explains what the purpose of the gift of speaking in tongues was all about. Ok so, this verse says that, tongues are for a sign, and it says that, that sign is not for the believers, oh boy, did you get that, did you understand that? Oh man, this is not good for the people who believe in speaking in tongues, you know, because I mean, they believe that speaking in tongues is a sign for those who believe, you know, for those who are saved, but this verse is saying exactly the opposite of that, you know, this verse says that speaking in tongues is not a sign for those who do believe, but, it's actually a sign for those who don't believe. I mean, what, what does this verse mean that it's a sign for those who don't believe, you may ask? Well, what this verse means is that, speaking in tongues was given so the disciples could go out and preach the gospel to other nations that spoke different languages, and in order for the disciples to be able to properly and or effectively communicate the word of God to those other nations, God gave them the ability to speak in tongues (different languages) as the Holy Ghost gave them utterance, which means, as the Holy Ghost told them what to say.

Ok so, do you get it now, do you understand this verse now, I hope you do, because this verse is as plain and or simple as could be, there's no trickery here, you know, it was written very straight forward, it means exactly what it says. You know, this makes me wonder, how could millions of Christians read this verse and still believe that speaking in tongues means what they think it means, you know, how could millions of Christians continue to believe that speaking in tongues (especially the way they practice it and speak it) means evidence of salvation, when this verse clearly says otherwise. I mean, I just don't get it, I just don't understand it, I just don't understand how this practice could be going on for almost hundred years now, because that's how long it's been going on (just Google it and read the interesting story of how it started, I was gonna write about how it started in this book, but I would rather you search it out for yourself, so you can get the whole story of it). I mean, I don't know, what's really going on, why are people continuing to practice a doctrine that is not Biblical, are they not reading these same verses, or are they just ignoring these verses and sticking to the ones that kinda maybe might mean what they want them to mean, you know, so they can justify their false doctrine. I mean, I still don't get it, I still don't get why people who seem to really love the Lord, people who seem to really want to obey the word of God, people who seem to really want to live a righteous life, I still don't get it why they would continue to practice a doctrine that is totally not Biblical. I mean, I'm really having a hard time understanding why and or how could Christians be so blind to the truth, you know, how could they read these scriptures and just totally misinterpret them. And the worth part is, how could they allow themselves to speak in gibberish thinking that they are actually speaking a spiritual language, I mean, come on somebody please help me with this, because I am really having a hard time understanding this. And the reason why I'm having a hard time understanding this is because, some of these people who believe in speaking in tongues are people who have PHDs in theology, you know, they are supposed to be scholars on the Bible, you know what I mean? And I mean, sure of course just because somebody has a PHD doesn't mean that they know it all, but I mean, if you have a PHD doesn't that mean that you have really examined the subject matter that you got that PHD in, you know, so that would mean that PHD person should kinda have a pretty good understanding of the subject matter. But you know what, when it comes to the Bible, it doesn't really matter if somebody has a PHD or not, because actually if your spiritual eyes and ears are not open, it is very easy for you not to understand what the verses are really saying, you know, your discernment of them can really be off, and I think this might be what is going on with the people who believe in speaking in tongues.

I mean, I don't know, but something bad is really going on here (with people who believe in speaking in tongues), and this something bad I believe has to do with the devil. And what I mean is, I believe that the devil is keeping these people's spiritual eyes and ears closed, you know, I believe that the devil is blinding the eyes and ears of the people who believe in speaking in tongues to where they can't see the truth about what speaking in tongues really means. And the reason why I say this is because, the people who believe in speaking in tongues want so much to believe in it that the devil blinds them to the truth, and not only that, I believe the devil gives them the utterance part of it, you know, gives them the gibberish speaking of it. And this is why it is so hard for the people who believe in speaking in tongues to stop believing in it, and it's because the devil has given them the utterance of gibberish (to serve as a sign) which comes out of them without effort and most often without even themselves anticipating it, you know, it comes out subconsciously. And this is why if you happen to attend a church serve that believes in speaking in tongues, this is why you will hear people shouting out gibberish out of nowhere, and it's because the devil brings it out of them as a way to keep them feeling like they are speaking in a spiritual language that just comes out of them without even they themselves making an effort to do it, which keeps the believer feeling special, you know, feeling like they are filled with the Holy Ghost, but in actuality it's the devil making them speak that way.

Now, you probably wanna ask me, how do I know, or why do I say it's the devil that makes them speak that way? And the reason why I say this is because, if it's not from God, then it's most likely from the devil, you know what I mean? I mean, if the power that is giving them the utterance is not from God, then it's most likely from the devil, you know, because like the Bible says, the devil is the author of confusion, you know, he is the father of lies. And so, since the doctrine of speaking in tongues is a false doctrine, who do you think got all these Christians who seem to really love the Lord to practice a doctrine that don't really make sense (confusion)? That's right, it's that ole lying serpent the devil, that's who! I mean, what do you think, who do you think has gotten all these millions of Christians to continue to practice a false doctrine for almost hundred years now? No really, I want to know? I mean, if you don't think the devil has his hands all over the speaking in tongues confusion, who or what makes the believers of it not seeing the truth, you know, why can't they see the true meaning of speaking in tongues. And the reason why they can't see it is because the devil has succeeded in blinding their spiritual eyes and ears from the truth. And the reason why he keeps succeeding in it is because the people who believe in it like it so much that they don't really want to accept maybe it might be false, thereby the devil continues to give them the ability to speak in gibberish, which makes the believer feel special. And the reason why I say that the devil gives them the ability to speak in gibberish is because, I really believe that the people who practice speaking in tongues are not faking it, you know, I really believe that the utterance actually just comes out of them without them actually consciously making themselves do it, you know, I really don't believe they are faking it (now some of them probably do be faking it, but I believe most of them are not), because if they are, then that would make their whole thanking, praising and worshipping of God nothing but vanity (meaning useless or for nothing).

And so yeah, we gonna need to really pray for people who believe in speaking in tongues, because the devil has really got a strong hold on them with this doctrine, you know, they are in a really terrible situation. And why I say they are in a terrible situation is because, in one hand they do really love the Lord, but on the other hand they have allowed the devil to corrupt their thanking, praising and worshipping of God by practicing a doctrine that is totally not Biblical. I mean it's crazy, but these people are really blinded and their spiritual ears are really blocked. And the reason why I say this is because, their manner of movement and the way that they utter their gibberish is pretty much the same way that other practitioners of strange doctrines utter their gibberish and move as well. And what I mean by this is, the way the believer moves and speaks when they speak in tongues is the same way that a lot of other people move and speak when they are practicing their strange religions. And one religion in particular, the Voodoo religion, the people who practice that religion pretty much have almost the same mannerism in movement and almost speak the same way (in their services) that the people who practice speaking in tongues do.

I mean, it's crazy, but just go on Youtube and type in "voodoo worship" and check it out, it's scary, it's crazy and it's very sad. And the reason why it's scary, crazy and very sad is because, the people who believe in speaking in tongues are Christians, you know, they are followers of Jesus Christ, you know, so for them to get caught up in that type of spiritual confusion is very sad, and this is why we must really pray for them, you know, so God can deliver them out of speaking in tongues doctrine, which is nothing more than the trick of the devil. And why you may want to ask would the devil want to trick Christians in such a way, well, the devil will use whatever tool and or opportunity to deceive people whenever possible. And the reason he does it is because his whole mission is to get as many people either away from God and or to get as many people to be corrupted in the way they thank, praise and worship God, you know, because he knows that God wants us to thank, praise and worship Him in truth and a pure heart. And so the devil looks to either confuse, trick, or other ways to get people to be corrupted in how we practice our Christianity. And so in this case, the people who believe in speaking in tongues have subconsciously allowed the devil to deceive them by accepting the doctrine as truth, and the devil works to make sure that they not only continue in their lost ways, but he works to get them to get other people to join them in their lost ways. And the real tragedy of this situation is that, this doctrine teaches their followers that they are not really saved until they can speak in tongues, thereby making their followers pray extra hard for the ability, you know, not knowing that the ability will be coming from the devil, not from God, you know, because it's not Biblical.

Man, I really don't know what else to say about this, I mean, it's gonna be real hard to convince and or to get the people who believe in speaking in tongues to give up their doctrine, you know, because they are so used to it and they are so comfortable in it that it's gonna pretty much take a miracle to get them to give it up. And the reason why they are so comfortable in it is because they have pretty much grown up on it, you know, from their grandfathers to their kids, you know, whole families have grown up on it, so to them, it's a natural thing, you know, it's part of what they have always known and or believed, you know, it's been past down from generation to generation, you known what I mean? And so to ask them to give it up is like asking them to abandon who they are, you know, it's like asking them to abandon the doctrine of their fathers and grandfathers, which can be really tough to do. And this is why most often times you will tend to see a very few people leave the churches that practice the speaking in tongues doctrine (you know when they finally realize it's not Biblical), and this is because leaving the church usually means pretty much abandoning your whole family, you know, because most speaking in tongues believing churches tend to be multi family oriented churches, you know, where most of the members belong to families that pretty much grow up in the churches, you know, from kids to grown-ups, they all pretty much grow up together, and so leaving the church will be pretty much like abandoning your own family, which can be very sad.

And so yeah, it's gonna be very tough to convince them to abandon their doctrine, but, a wrong is a wrong, and the Bible does say it is good for correction, and so I myself will try to get the conversation on this really started, because I haven't heard much discussed on this topic, and so somebody has got to get it started in a real way. And I mean, this is one of the main reasons I decided to write this book, and it's because I just can't fathom how millions of Christians can allow themselves to be deceived by the devil like this, especially the people in the leadership positions at these churches, because truth be told most people in the congregations whole heartedly are not that spiritual aware, you know, they pretty much just follow (blindly) what their church leaders teach them, and so it's very easy for them to be deceived. But, I just don't understand how the church leaders can be this blind, I mean, come on, can somebody please wake up already, I mean, can somebody please wake them up already. Oh well I guess all we can do is pray for them and hopefully God will wake them up sooner than later, you know, hopefully before their new generation (who are kids right now) end up growing up to continue the cycle of practice speaking in tongues. But you know what, with God nothing is impossible, and I am going to right now speak it into existence that God will deliver them from the hands of the devil within this generation (I think a generation is what, about 20 0r 30 years). So come on my fellow Christians, I invite you to join me in this "End of Speaking in Tongues Movement" that I'm about to start as soon as this book comes out. No, I'm serious, email me for more info, and I'll let you know what the plan is (I haven't really come up with one right now as I'm writing this, lol, but I'm sure I'll have one by the time this book is done, or if I don't, maybe you will have one, then you can just share that with me, and we can join forces, in Jesus's name).

Ok, so, I think that is all I really have for this chapter, and I know there's a lot more verses about speaking in tongues that I didn't go over them, but this verse has just put a stop to my need and or aim to check out all the verses that talks about tongue or tongues, you know, which was what I initially wanted to do, and was tirelessly doing until I ran into this verse; **1 Corinthians 14:22**, which has put a halt to my aim, because this verse was just so clear in its wording, you know, the meaning was just starring right at my heart, you know, almost like it was saying to me: **"ok that's it, you do not need to search any more, I'm gonna put it to you as plainly as possible, so your heart can be comforted that your discerning of the scriptures to get to the truth of whether the speaking in tongues doctrine is Biblical or not, you have seeked the truth and it has been shown to you, now that's it, you have done your due diligence in this matter, now go on and move on to writing the next chapter of this book."**

And so my friends, that's it, I have no more to say about this chapter, but I want to encourage you to go ahead and check out all the verses that speak about tongue or tongues and if you find any verse that may contradict this verse please let me know, because I'm here to learn and to seek the truth, as we all should be, as we strive to be better Christians. And let the church say, Amen!

6

GOSPEL MUSIC

Is it just me or is gospel music nowadays starting to sound more and more like secular music? And the reason why I ask this is because, it seems like to me, it seems like every time I tune into a gospel radio station (usually when I'm in the car and in the mood for some gospel music), it seems like I keep hearing more and more songs that sound just like secular songs. And when I say sounds like, I'm not just talking about the beats (the instrumentals), I'm talking about even the lyrics and or how the verses are sang and or performed. I mean it's crazy, but sometimes I can't even understand what the artist is saying and or what the song is really about! I mean, it's almost like these artists are not sure whether they want to do gospel music or secular music, you know what I mean? You know what, I think I know why a lot of gospel music nowadays tend to sound a lot like secular music, and the reason is, I believe it's because there's a lot of gospel artists who really deep down want to be secular artists but for whatever reason they are stuck doing gospel music, and therefore their gospel songs end up sounding more and more like secular songs, and that is because that is where their musical spirit really is, you know, in secular music. I mean, what do you think, am I right or wrong? And this is why gospel artist have to make sure that gospel music is really what they want to do, you know, that way their music is not corrupted by secular influences. And the reason why I say this is because, gospel music is supposed to be created to thank, praise and or worship the Lord, and so if that's the case, it needs to be as pure as possible, and adding any secular influences to it can easily taint it and or corrupt it, which will make the music pretty much useless in the sight of the Lord, which will mean the music was created in vain, meaning it was created for no real Holy purpose, but instead it was maybe created for entertainment, which is a no no for gospel music.

Now, don't get me wrong, I don't mean to suggest that gospel music can't be exciting and make the listener want to move, jump, shout and etc., as they become filled with joy from the music, oh no, that's not what I'm saying. And what I'm saying is, the focal point in making gospel music should be to thank, praise and worship God with the music, then if the music make the people extra excited to where they want to move and shout, that's fine, there's nothing wrong with that. And the reason why I'm saying all of this is because there seems to be a lot of gospel songs that seem to have been created more so for making people move and shout (entertainment) than for praising and worshipping God. And this is why a lot of gospel songs tend to have samples of secular songs (whether the beat or phrases) in them. And the reason for that is so the songs can be not only more entertaining, but also so the songs can have more of a crossover appeal, you know, so the songs can appeal to both the gospel world and the secular world. Now, don't get me wrong here either, there's nothing wrong with wanting gospel songs to appeal to the secular world, oh no, not at all, and actually, it would be fantastic if more and more gospel songs did crossover and appealed to the secular world, because that would mean that more and more people in the secular world would get a chance to hear about the greatness of God and Jesus Christ on a regular basis, which could greatly influence them in wanting to become Christians and or to become better Christians. And so there's nothing wrong with wanting gospel songs to penetrate through the secular world, but, the sampling of secular songs into gospel music in order to make the gospel songs more appealing to the secular world is a no no, not good at all. And the reason why it's no good is because, every song that is created carries a spirit in it, you know, like for example; some songs carry the spirit of fornication, and other songs may carry the spirit of criminality, and other songs may carry the spirit of murder, and other songs may carry the spirit of idolatry, and so on and so on. And so for example; if a gospel artist samples a secular song that was about fornication and mixes that into their gospel song that is about praising and worshipping God, the spirit of the secular song will corrupt the gospel song and render the gospel song unholy (which is what gospel songs should be).

    I mean,, are you understanding what I'm trying to say here, because I feel like I'm not doing such a good job of explaining it, but umm, ok, let me try again to explain. And what I'm trying to say is, samples of songs (whether beat or phrase) carry with them the spirit of the whole song, and so a sample of a secular song carries with it the spirit of the whole secular song. And so it's like, a sample of a secular song (whether beat or phrase) that talks about fornication carries with it the spirit of fornication, and so therefore when that sample is mixed into a gospel song, that sample taints and or corrupts the gospel song by injecting the spirit of fornication into the gospel song, which turns the gospel song to being unclean and or not pure. And I'm pretty sure you know why gospel songs need to be pure, right? I mean if you don't, then I would strongly suggest you open up the Bible and start doing some serious………., ok, you know what, it would probably be easier if I just told you why, right, since I already have your an divided attention, and since you seem like a real nice person, and since I'm the author here and I'm supposed to be telling you about the Bible, right, lol, ok, I got you, let's continue!

    Ok, anyway so, the reason why gospel songs need to be pure is because that is what God requires from us, you know, He requires that anything we present to Him should be pure, you know, it should be without blemish, as the Bible says; Leviticus 22:20 **"But whatsoever hath a blemish, that shall ye not offer: for it shall not be acceptable for you."** Leviticus 22:21 **"And whosoever offereth a sacrifice of peace offerings unto the LORD to accomplish his vow, or a freewill offering in beeves or sheep, it shall be perfect to be accepted; there shall be no blemish therein."** So you see, God demands that anything we present to Him should be pure, and this is also the reason why He brought us Jesus Christ, you know, it's so Jesus can purify us and make us pure in the sight of God.

Ok, so, do you get it now, do you understand it now, I hope you do, because this is the best I can explain it. So if you are an artist please make sure any gospel songs you do are pure, you know, that way not only can the songs be acceptable to God, but also, so that way when some of us Hip Hop heads who are trying to be better Christians tune into gospel radio stations to hear some gospel music, instead of us hearing songs that sound just like the secular songs we listen to on a regular basis, it would be nice to tune in on a gospel radio station and zone out on the great gospel songs that thank, praise and worship God without being distracted by samples of secular songs. And what I mean by distracted is, for example; you could be listening to a nice gospel song that is praising God, but then you hear a sample of a popular secular song in the song, then what happens is, instead of your mind concentrating on praising God through the song, your mind starts to shift into trying to remember what the secular song was that the sample comes from and what the secular song was talking about. I mean it's like, I once heard a gospel song that had a sample of Marvin Gaye's "Sexual Healing" song, I think the sample was just part of the beat, but I quickly recognized the sample, and by recognizing the sample, instead of my mind staying focused on praising God through the song, my mind instead started wondering and or thinking about sexual healing, you know, as I kept hearing the sample. And so this is one of the reasons why it's important for gospel songs to not sample secular songs, and it's because it can easily distract the listener from concentrating on praising God through the song, by making them to start thinking of the secular song that the sample came from.

Ok, so, I think that is all I really wanted to say about gospel music, and that is it should be pure, that way some of us who are trying to be better Christians can enjoy the songs (when we are in our spiritual moments) without having to be reminded of the secular world that we spend most of our time in, you know what I mean!?

Oh, wait a minute, I almost forgot, but I actually got one more thing that I want to touch on about gospel music, and that thing is: the Awards, you know, the awards that are given to gospel artists, you know, like the "Stellar" and the "Dove" awards that are given each year to gospel artists that are supposed to recognize them as being the best gospel artists of the year and or something like that. And what I'm trying to say is, why are we giving out awards to people for making songs to thank, praise and worship God? I mean, since when did thanking, praising and worshipping God become a competition? I mean, why are we giving statues to people for making songs about the greatness of God, because I mean, isn't that borderline idolatry? And the reason why I say its borderline idolatry is because, the Bible warns us so many times in the verses about not creating statues and idolizing them, you know, because that is almost like worshipping the statues, and you know how God feels about idol worshipping, right? And so why would we think it's ok to make statues and give them to people who make songs about the greatness of God? I mean, that has got to be almost like an abomination in the sight of God, you know what I mean? I mean it's crazy, but every time I see a gospel awards show I can't help but think why are we giving each other awards for thanking, praising and worshipping God, because I mean, isn't that what we are supposed to be doing anyway (whether we are doing it as a ministry or not, which is what being a gospel artist really is, it's a ministry, you know, it's a music ministry).

I mean, I don't know, but the whole thing of giving people awards for praising God just doesn't sit so well with me, what do you think? No really, I really want to know what you think on this, because I've never heard anybody raise any issues with it before, so I really want to know your opinion on this, so email me please and let me know, so maybe we can start a real dialog on this (giving each other awards issue) and see if it's borderline idolatry or not, and if it is, then see if we can start a movement to end it!

Now, I don't see anything wrong if gospel artists wanna get together to praise God and appreciate each other for the hard work they put in to create great songs that thank, praise and worship God, nah, I don't see anything wrong with that, you know, just as long as it doesn't turn into a competition, which is what awards shows are all about, you know, deciding who are the best (the winners) and who are not the best (those who don't win any awards). Now, you probably want to ask me, if we shouldn't give each other awards, then how can we show appreciation to each other for the hard work we put in to create great songs that people can use to thank, praise and worship God with. Well my friends, I actually got a solution to this dilemma, and the solution is; everyone who makes a gospel song that year should receive an award, and that award should be "A Certificate of Appreciation" award, or, "A Certificate of Participation" award, you know, just like how they do in youth activities, you know, where everybody gets an award just for participating, you know what I mean? I mean is this a great idea or what? And the reason why I think it's a great idea is because, not only will that satisfy people's need for recognition and or desire to feel appreciated (which is why people love to receive awards), but the idea will also eliminate the perception that there's competition in gospel music (which is what giving of awards deciding who is the best singer, or best songwriter, or etc., represents), which it should not be. And the reason why I say this is because, I'm pretty sure in God's eyes there's no such thing as one gospel song being better than another gospel song. And I'm pretty sure in God's eyes there's no such thing as one singer being better than another singer. And so in God's eyes all songs that are created to honor Him that are pure are the best songs of the year, no matter whether those songs are well written and or well sang or not, you know, it's the intent of the song that matters, not the production of it, you know what I mean?

And so yeah, give everyone certificates of appreciation, you know, for contributing songs that thank, praise and worship God. And if certificates are not good enough appreciation for them, than maybe gospel music is not for them, you know, maybe they should go ahead and do secular music, you know, where anything goes, and where awards and idolizations are tremendously promoted and or craved. And the reason why I'm saying this is because, as the Bible says; KJV-Mark 12:17 **"And Jesus answering said unto them, Render to Caesar the things that are Caesar's, and to God the things that are God's. And they marvelled at him."** And so in this case, secular music is Caesar's and gospel music is God's, you know what I mean? And so if you are a gospel artist, your music is created to honor God, and so you don't need men to honor you for the good job you are doing to honor God, because to do so can greatly increase the focus on you, and in turn reduce the focus on God, which is what gospel music is supposed to do, you know, make us focus and or feel closer to God. I mean, are you understanding what I'm trying to say here? And what I'm really trying to say is, gospel music is not for gaining fame and fortune (that's what the secular music industry is for, lol), no, nope, gospel music is for honoring God. And so the less honoring of ourselves for creating gospel songs, the more God will receive the glory. And so, sure there's nothing wrong with us appreciating each other for creating great songs that honor God, but we shouldn't do it to the point where we are giving each other statues (which is borderline idolatry) and all sorts of other awards that do nothing but diminish the pureness and or the purpose of us creating those great gospel songs in the first place.

And so yeah, gospel music is about honoring God, and so let's try our best to keep it pure, which is what God requires we do of anything that we present to Him, you know what I mean? Alright, that's all I got for this chapter, I hope you understood what I was trying to say, but if not, just send me an email and we can discuss some more, ok, alright, cool, be blessed!

7

HOMOSEXUALITY

When I was about 11 years old there used to be this young boy neighbor of ours that used to act very feminine. I think he was about 13 or 14 years old. I used to always wonder why he acted like that, you know, I used to wonder why he acted like a girl. I used to hear rumors that he was gay, you know, I used to hear rumors that he would engage in sexual relations with men. I remember I used to feel very sorry for him, and wondered why and or how he ended up like that, especially in such a young age. I mean, I just could not understand, I just could not fathom and or believe that he was actually gay, you know, I just couldn't believe that he was ok with sleeping with men. And the reason why I had such a hard time understanding it is because, I just couldn't imagine and or see why would a guy want to sleep with another guy, you know, I just couldn't understand why a guy would want to sleep with another guy instead of sleeping with a woman, you know what I mean? And so I used to just look at him and just wonder why, and or just wonder how he got that way. I never really got to know him that well, I mean, we never really played together and or talked to each other much, even though he lived right next door to us. He lived just him and his father, and he used to be gone from their place almost the whole day and would come back just in time before his father would get home. But, there were numerous times that he would come back home after his father got there and he would get in big trouble, and when I say big trouble, I'm talking about his father would ask him where he has been, and why the chores where not done, and before you know it his father would proceed to beat the heck out of the boy.

I mean, it was scary, it was horrifying when he would get the beatings, because not only would the boy be screaming at the top of his lungs (almost sounding like he's about to die as he screamed and as he tried to catch his breath), but you could pretty much hear the sound of the belt as it hit the boy's body. And sometimes his father would make the boy go outside and get a stick for the father to use to beat the boy with, and often I could see the boy shaking as he was outside looking for a stick. Then, a few minutes later as he would go back inside with the stick, all you could hear is the father shouting at the boy as he hit him with the stick, and you could hear the boy screaming in pain as he was being whipped. I mean it was crazy, a lot of times you could actually hear the stick breaking from the force of the beating. A lot of times I actually thought the father was going to beat the boy to death. And a lot of times I wished I was big enough to go and stop the father from beating his son like that, you know, because he beat his son like he didn't love and or even like his own son.

I mean, a lot of times I just wondered why the father couldn't just send the son to his mother, you know, maybe his mother would be the better person to raise the boy than the father, you know what I mean? But then again, I'm guessing the mother probably sent the son to live with his father so his father could man him up, you know, put some discipline on the boy and get the boy to act more like a man then a girl. I really think that is what happened I think the mother recognized the gay tendencies in the boy and decided to send the boy to his father for some man training, you know what I mean? And I think the father noticed the gay tendencies in his son and did not know how to handle it, and as a result ended up putting an extra beating on his son not just for coming home late and or for not doing choirs, I think he put those extra beatings more so because his son had gay tendencies and his father couldn't handle having a gay son, so as a result he subconsciously beat his son unmercifully, you know, almost like he was trying to beat the gay out of his son, you know what I mean?

I mean it was crazy, and I used to think to myself, why wouldn't the boy just make sure that he did his chores on time, you know, make sure the chores are done before the father got home. And I used to wonder where does the boy go to the whole day (when school was out or after school) to be coming home late in the evening. I mean that whole experience (him being beat and him screaming like that) pretty much left me traumatized to beatings and people crying. I mean even up to this day, I have a really hard time with seeing and or hearing people crying, especially children, I just can't handle it. And this is why I thank God that my kids are pretty much well behaved, and when they kinda get out of line, a stern talking to usually gets the job done, you know, it gets them back in line. And I mean, I did have to whip them a few times before (when they were younger), but that was pretty hard for me to do, but I had to man up and do it, you know, so they can learn that there is serious consequence to serious misbehavior, you know, but it was hard for me to whip them, and it was even harder for me to hear them crying afterward, because every time they cried, it felt like my soul was being tortured one tear drop at a time. But that is what you have to do as a parent sometimes, you know, sometimes you gotta let your kids know that serious misbehavior will not be tolerated, and sometimes nothing can say that better than a whipping, especially if they are not used to being whipped, an occasional whipping can really wake them up to the seriousness of the matter that should not be repeated by them anymore.

Now, notice how I said occasional whipping, and the reason why I said that is because, whipping your kids all the time does nothing but diminish the power of a whipping. And what I mean by that is, if you whoop your kids all the time, over time your kids will get used to being whipped, and therefor instead of them being scared to do something stupid in fear of they might get a whooping, they instead become more hard headed because they lose the fear of getting a whipping, you know, because they become so used to getting a whipping that the whipping don't faze them anymore, you know, they become immune to it, you know what I mean? And this is why a lot of parents who use whipping their kids as the main discipline tactic end up getting frustrated when the whooping don't seem to work, and it's because their kids have become so used to it that it almost becomes like a game, you know, of who can handle a whipping better kinda of thing, you know what I mean? And this is one of the reasons how parents can easily find themselves abusing their kids, and it's because they think they have to beat their kids extra hard, you know, so as to make their kids feel the pain from the beating, but, all the parent is really doing here is make their kids hate them more and more, as their kids come to see their parents as not loving parents, but abusers. And so it can be very tricky when it comes to disciplining kids using whipping as a discipline method, because if it is not used properly, all you gonna do is traumatize your kids by abusing them, which in turn will either make them act up some more or make them learn to fear you, which in turn will result in them thinking that you don't love them, which in turn will make them grow up to either resent you and or to hate you.

And so anyway, yeah, that boy's father used to beat the heck out of him, and I used to feel very sorry for him. And I truly believe that the beating were made more severe because of the son's gay tendencies, you know, because fathers just have an extra hard time accepting that their son is actually gay, you know, most fathers just can't really handle it. And to make matters worse, his father was a military guy, you know, he was this big six foot tall muscular military guy that was the portrait of toughness, you know what I mean? I mean, he was one of those big tough looking guys that no one would dare want to mess with, you know what I mean? And so I'm pretty sure the idea that his son might be gay just would not have settled well with him, you know, especially with him being a military guy on top of all that. And not only that, but this was in the mid-1980s, you know, when being gay was still a big taboo in most of the world, especially in Africa (and this is where this story I'm telling now is taking place), you know, where being gay was looked open as being the worst dirty sin ever, you know what I mean? And so no father at that time would be able to handle and or accept that their son is a homosexual, oh no, no way, I can't see it. I mean, even now (in 2016), it is still very hard for fathers to really accept that their sons may be gay, you know, they just can't do it, you know, they just can't. And the reason why fathers have a hard time accepting it is because, to fathers, their sons are their little mini me, you know, their sons are pretty much extensions of themselves, you know, their sons are like their little warriors that are here to carry on their fathers, their grandfathers, their great grandfathers, and their great great grandfathers name and or traditions, you know what I mean? And so, it becomes very hard for fathers to accept that their little mini me, their little warrior that they expected to grow up to be strong, tough, manly man, who will carry the family name forward with manly pride, they have a hard time accepting that their little warrior has instead grown up to be strong, tough, girly man who will carry the family name forward with gay pride, you know what I mean? And what I mean is, fathers just have a hard time seeing their boys act like girls, you know, because fathers see their boys as little manly extensions of themselves, and so for their boys to turn out to be gay is just too hard for fathers to accept. And this is why a lot of boys who come out the closet end up losing their relationships with their fathers, and it's because their fathers just can't bring themselves to accept the fact that their sons are gay, you know, it is just too painful for fathers to have to deal with it, and as a result, their fathers will most likely just distance themselves from their sons, and may even go as far as to shun their sons, you know, end up kicking their sons out the house and pretend that their sons no longer exist, you know, pretend their sons are dead to them. And this is why you will tend to see gay boys or gay men be much closer to their mothers than their fathers, and it's because mothers tend to be a little bit more accepting of their sons being gay then fathers do. And the reason why mothers tend to be a little bit more accepting is because, mothers generally are nurturers by nature, you know, and so they have more of an ability to sympathize with their kids than fathers do, you know what I mean?

And so yeah, fathers just have a hard time accepting that their kids may be gay, and I'm suspecting that was what was going on with that boy's father, and as a result, he ended up giving his son unnecessary extra beats just because he couldn't deal with the fact that his son was indeed gay. I mean it was crazy though, and come to think of it I actually feel sorry for both of them, the father and the son. And the reason why I feel sorry for both of them is because, there they were, just the two of them, father and son, who instead of learning how to understand each other, and or instead of taking the time to learn how to have a good relationship with each other, you know, so they could enjoy a healthy father son relationship, they instead became the source of each other's misery and torment, you know, the father is tormented by the fact that his son may be gay, and the son is miserable because he feels like his father not only does not understand him, but he is tormented by the fact that his father is choosing to beat the crap out of him instead of trying to understand him. So the whole thing was just so unfortunate, because really, the father was not really a bad person, I mean, he did have a tough exterior, but for the most part he just kept to himself and was friendly to the people around him. I mean, I never knew him that well, but he was always nice to me, I mean, he would always ask me how I was doing whenever he say me sitting on the front porch by myself day dreaming about life and how I'm gonna become rich when I grow up, lol. But yeah, he was real nice to me, and actually, one time he even carried me to the hospital when I had burned my foot badly playing around and not paying attention. And when I say carried me to the hospital, I mean he literally throw me on his shoulders and carried me all the way to the hospital by foot, yes, by foot. The good thing is the hospital was not that far from where we lived, but it was still a good distance away by foot, I mean, I think it was at least 30 or 40 minutes away by foot. And he walked that whole distance with me on his shoulders without even taking a break, I mean, I don't even remember him changing shoulders or nothing like that, all I remember is him saying "it's ok, you gonna be alright, we are almost at the hospital", something like that. I mean, I will never forget that episode, and I will forever be grateful to him for doing that for me. Now, you are probably wondering how the how episode happened, right, you are probably wondering how I really ended up burning my foot, right, ok, I'mma tell you. And what had happen was, me and my brother were outside running around chasing each other (I thing we were playing tag), then I remember me running around this hole on the ground where the people used to throw away their ashes from the charcoal or something like that (this was in Africa when I was 11 years old in the mid-1980s), and then what happened was I did not notice how extra close I was to the hole, because the next thing I knew was I slipped and started falling into the hole.

The hole was not that deep, but it was deep enough (taller than I was) and it was full of ashes (which came almost up to my knees), and it seems like those ashes were just thrown in there not that long ago, because as soon as my feet hit the bottom, I could feel them burning with intense heat, I mean, my feet felt like they were in the actual fire from the charcoal. My brother started laughing at first thinking that I was playing around, but he quickly realized I was actually being burned by the ashes, so he quickly extended his hand so he could pull me back up, but we struggled a little bit because I couldn't find any hard surface to place my footing, but then I moved to a narrower spot on the whole and he was able to pull me back up out of the hole. All I remember after that is me running as fast as I could all the way home (we were about 15 minutes from home), when I got home no one was there, my first instinct was to find some Vaseline and put a bunch on there, which did nothing but intensify the burning pain in both of my feet (especially my right foot which got burnt the most), I mean it felt like I had just added gasoline to my foot when I put the Vaseline on it, to which point I let out some loud screams of pain, and this is when our next door neighbor came running in to see what was going on. Then next thing I know, as soon as he saw my foot, he told my brother to hang tight he was gonna take me to the hospital and then proceeded to throw me on his shoulders and started walking to the hospital. Now, this was in Africa in the 1980s, so there was no such thing as calling an ambulance or nothing like that, the most you could do is call a taxi, and even that was tricky, because most taxis stayed downtown, and not to mention the cost of a taxi. And so most people when they got real sick, they just had to take their time and walk to the hospital or to the nearest clinic if one was around.

And so yeah, that dude actually carried me all the way to the hospital, so to me, he wasn't really a bad guy, he just did not know how to handle his son having gay tendencies or his son being actually gay, as most fathers can't. But, your kids are your kids, and sometimes your kids will just find themselves caught up in situations that even they themselves don't know and or don't understand how they got in that predicament. And the reason why I say predicament is because, I truly don't believe that gay people actually consciously chose to be gay, and what I mean by that is, I truly don't believe that gay people just wake up one morning and decide, you know what, I don't want to be heterosexual any more, from now on I want to be gay. And what I'm talking about here is not gay people finally coming out of the closet, no, I'm talking about when a gay person finally comes to the realization that maybe they might actually be gay after all. And this is what I mean by finding themselves in the predicament, and the predicament is; they find themselves not really attracted to the opposite sex, but instead they find themselves attracted to their same sex, you know, men attracted to other men, and women attracted to other women. And so now, the predicament is; should they come out the closet or not, you know, should they embrace their reality of being attracted to their same sex and live a life of homosexuality, or, should they stay in the closet and try to force themselves to live a life of heterosexuality? Now, the easiest decision is probably to stay in the closet and try to live a life of heterosexuality. And the reason why I say this is probably the easiest decision for them is because, for one, they wouldn't have to go through all that shame, scrutiny and or hatred that they may have to deal with for living as an openly gay person. And the reason why they may have to face shame, scrutiny and or hatred is because for the most part the world is still pretty much homophobic. And I mean, most western countries (the U.S, Europe and others) do try their best to pass laws to protect the gay community for harm and or hatred, but for the majority of the countries in the world, homosexuality is still an extremely taboo lifestyle, you know, to where an openly gay person can easily find themselves being tremendously harassed and or killed. And so this is why staying in the closet may be an easier decision for them than to come out, you know, so they won't have to face all that shame, scrutiny and or hatred that is sure to follow them. And so also, the other reason why staying in the closet may be an easier decision than to come out is because, they know that their families will have a hard time dealing with and or accepting them as being gay, you know, they know that if they come out that might mean they will lose a lot of family members, you know, they know that their families might end up alienating them and or they know that their families may not want to have anything to do with them anymore.

attention to the person that came and sat next to me on the seat. When the person sat down I slightly moved over so as to give them more room on the seat. I think I had my headphones on listening to music from my Walkman, but then, not long after the person sat down, I felt a hand on my thigh, so I looked down on my thigh, and sure enough, the guy sitting next to me had placed his hand on my thigh. I mean, I froze for a few seconds there in disbelief, I mean, I was trying to figure out whether he mistook my thigh for his, or did he intentionally place his hand on my thigh. I mean it was so weird, I really couldn't believe it, so I turned around and looked at him with a stern quizzical look on my face like, what the heck are you doing with your hand on my thigh kinda look. He just sat there staring at me for a few more seconds before removing his hand. I did not know what to think about the whole thing, I mean, he really caught me by surprise. I started to think, should I punch him and or elbow him on his jaw right there and then, or should I just let it go. I chose to just let it go, and I just got up and moved to another seat. But I just couldn't get my mind of the whole situation, you know, for a stranger to just put their hand on my thigh, I mean, come on, really!?

And so anyway, yeah, it's not that hard for a person to be exposed to the spirit of homosexuality, and if the person happens to be unsure of their sexuality, they become very vulnerable to succumbing to the spirit of homosexuality entering them. And once the spirit of homosexuality enters a person, it becomes very hard for that person to fight it and or remove it from inside of them. I mean it's crazy, but the spirit of homosexuality is very strong, and the only thing that can really get it out of a person is prayer, you know, you God can get the spirit out, but the person has to really want to get it out, and the person really has to go to God in prayer with a tremendous desire to be healed from it, and only God can do the healing. And when I say only God can do the healing, the reason why I say that is because, when it comes to spirits, we humans don't really have the strength to fight spirits, you know, because spirits operate in the supernatural arena, and we humans operate in the natural arena, and so to fight a spirit we pretty much need the assistance of God, and this is why we rely heavily on Jesus to be our shield and or protector from the supernatural spirits. I mean, are you understanding what I'm trying to say here? And what I'm trying to say is, we can't fight supernatural spirits with our natural powers, we pretty much need Jesus to give us the strength to be able to defeat the supernatural spirits (demons) that might be trying to attack us.

And so, I really want to urge the gay people out there that would like to be healed from the spirit of homosexuality to really become close to God, you know, to really pray that God would give them the strength to fight off the homosexual spirit that is possessing and or corrupting their minds to think and or feel that not only are they attracted to individuals of their same sex, but the spirit of homosexuality is also corrupting their minds to think that there's nothing wrong with being gay. Now, I know a lot of the people in the gay community will argue with me in saying this, but there is something wrong with being gay. And the wrong thing is, not only is it a sin in God's eyes, but it also totally goes against nature, you know, that is not how God and or nature (if you are not a God believing person) intended for us humans to be. And so, I can only imagine how much of a monumental task it could be to free yourself from the spirit of homosexuality, but with God, anything is possible. So if you are a gay person who truly wants to free yourself from the spirit of homosexuality, I would suggest you find a church that is not judgmental and get them to pray for and with you about it, so that way not only will you have a strong support team to help you in overcoming your homosexual spirit, but also so you can slowly start to build a one on one personal relationship with God, which in turn will give you extra strength to fight your homosexual spirit. I mean, it's not gonna be easy, but if you are sincere about becoming free from your homosexual bondage (and yes it is a bondage, because it is not normal, no matter how much the gay community tries to normalize it), God is still in the miracle business, and if you have Jesus in your life, there's nothing you can't overcome.

Now, I know there's gonna be a lot of people from the gay community that are not gonna agree with me over me saying that homosexuality is a bondage, but it is. And the reason why I say this is because, I truly don't believe that if given the choice to be heterosexual or homosexual I don't believe most gay people would still prefer to be homosexual, especially if they happen to be Christians and or believe in God. And the reason why I say this is because, there are a lot of gay folks who are Christians who would really like to be right with God, but they just can't seem to be able to fight and overcome their homosexual spirits. And this is why there seems to be a lot of Christians and or people who believe in God and the Bible who are gay nowadays, and it's because they just can't seem to fight and or overcome their homosexual spirits that has them in bondage, you know what I mean? I mean, I don't know, I could be wrong, but I just refuse to believe that most gay Christians or most gay people who believe in God don't know that God considers homosexuality a sin. I mean, what do you think, am I right or wrong? And so if I am right, then why would gay Christians and or gay people who believe in God continue to lead a lifestyle that is totally against God, you know, a lifestyle that God considers to be an abomination. And so this is why I say that gay folks are in bondage, and the only person that can really deliver them from this bondage is God himself, you know, through prayer and perseverance, and more prayer and perseverance.

And so yeah, homosexuality is a spirit, and the only way to fight it is through prayer, sincere prayer. But I know that most people in the gay community are not gonna like my saying here, because they have pretty much decided that they would rather lead a homosexual lifestyle than fight it. And this is why they are working so hard to try and normalize it, you know, this is why they are working so hard to make society accept it and or even embrace it, you know what I mean? And the reason why they are doing that is because, they don't really believe they can be freed from it, you know, they just find it easier to accept that they are gay and just go on and live their lives like there's nothing wrong with it. But there is something wrong with it, for one, it totally goes against nature, and for two, it totally goes against God's word the Bible. And the funny thing is (actually not funny, more like scary), there are gay preachers and or pastors nowadays, I mean, really, how did that happen. I mean, how do these gay preachers and or pastors are able to get that close to the word of God and not be afraid of going against God's word the Bible that they are holding in their hands and reading from it? I mean, I don't know how they can do that, I mean, how can they just ignore the verses that say laying with a man like he's a woman is an abomination, you know what I mean? I mean, how do they do that, how do they reconcile those verses that speak about abomination; you know what I'm saying? I mean, I don't know man, it seems like we are all just so screwed up in our understanding of scriptures that we just end up making up stuff and doing whatever we want to do with no regards of whether we being Biblical or not. It's crazy, and this is why I decided to call this book "Christianity Lost", and it's because it seems like we are really lost, I mean, it looks like we are really off the Reservations (so to speak), you know, almost like we are still wondering in the wilderness, you know, not know whether we coming or going. I mean, I don't know, but we got some serious issues in the Christian community, and the only way to solve them is gonna be by engaging in some serious dialogs that can not only shed light to these issues, but dialog that can also bring about some serious changes in how we practice our Christianity, because right now we are failing, we are failing to not only teach the truth, but we are failing to understand the truth, and that is why we are so lost and that is why we continue to be lost. But I for sure are gonna try my best to start the dialog, and hopefully there will be others who will be brave enough to join me. And the reason why I say brave enough is because, when it comes to beliefs, most people will fight you tooth and nail to try to discourage you from starting and or progressing a movement that can bring about real transformational enlightenment that speaks truth to power, especially if that truth goes against their beliefs, even if their beliefs are totally false.

But so anyway (back to our homosexuality topic), the only other thing I want to say about homosexuality is that, I truly believe that if a gay person truly wants to be free from it they can through prayer and perseverance of course. And also I want to say that, we in the heterosexual community should do our best not to judge and or bring any hard to our brothers and sisters in the gay community, because whether we accept and or agree with their lifestyle or not, those are still our brothers and sisters, and we should do our best to love them and to support them the best we can as they try to live their lives the best they know how. And so, sure, we don't have to agree with their lifestyle, and we don't have to support their aim to try to normalize their lifestyle, but trying to shame them and or bring harm to them is totally not acceptable. And I'm really trying to talk to the people that seem to be homophobic, you know, the people who seem to be a little bit overzealous in their rejection of homosexuality. Now, don't get me wrong, there's nothing wrong with stating that homosexuality is a sin and or un-natural, but to try to bring about shame to them by shouting out condemnations and or trying to oppress them is not productive. And so all you preachers out there that like to use derogatory speech in condemning gay folks please stop it, it does no good but actually can be the reason why most gay folks don't feel welcome in churches, a place that could probably help them gain strength to fight and or overcome their homosexual spirits.

Well, that's it my friends, that's all I have for this chapter, so let's please treat each other with kindness and respect, you know, because we are all brothers and sisters in the Lord, yes, even gay folks are our brothers and sisters in the Lord, so instead of trying to shame them for them to change their lifestyle, let's instead pray for them so they can not only have the courage to want to change their lifestyle, but so they can also have the strength to fight and overcome their homosexual spirit, you know, so that way they can be on the right side of the word of God, as what we all should be trying to be, you know what I mean? Ok, alright, can I get an Amen, thanks, Amen!!!

8

CHRISTMAS & EASTER

It was very weird not celebrating Christmas two days ago, yes, two days ago was December 25th and me and my wife and kids did not celebrate Christmas at all. And when I say at all, I mean, at all, nothing, you know, no Christmas tree, no lights decorations, no Christmas cards, no Christmas presents, nothing, nope, nothing at all. And the reason why we did not celebrate Christmas is because I finally searched out the true origins of Christmas and squared that up with what the Bible teaches about traditions and came to finally accept that Christmas is not really a holy day. And the reason why I say it's not really a holy day is because, the origins of Christmas are not holy at all, and the reason why they are not holy is because Christmas was originated from the pagans, you know, the people who used to worship idols back in the Bible days, and you know how God hates the worship of idols, right? And so, how Christmas got started is like this; the pagan people used to worship their sun-god Mithras's birthday on December 25th, and then so, when the Emperor Constantine (the emperor of Rome at the time, who was a pagan worshipper) converted to Christianity, he made Christianity the religion of the Roman Empire, and as he did so, and as the pagan people started converting into Christianity, they brought with them a lot of their pagan traditions into Christianity, including the December 25th birthday worship of their sun-god Mithras, which they adopted to serve as the birthday of Jesus Christ.

And so as you can see, December 25th is not even a holy day, it's pretty much an idol worship day, because that is the day the pagans used to worship and or celebrate the birth of their sun-god idol, and you know how God hates idol worshipping, right? And so there's no way December 25th can be a holy day, because we humans don't have the power to turn something that is not holy and make it holy, only God himself can do that. And this is why God brought us Jesus Christ, and it's so Jesus can turn us from being unholy in the sight of God to holy, you know, so God turned us holy himself through Jesus Christ, you know what I mean? And so there's no way can December 25th be holy, unless God himself turns it to be holy, and there's nowhere in the Bible that says December 25th is holy, and for the most part the Bible actually warns us about observing the traditions of men, as we read in the book of Mark 7:7-9 (KJV); **"Howbeit in vain do they worship me, teaching *for* doctrines the commandments of men. For laying aside the commandment of God, ye hold the tradition of men, *as* the washing of pots and cups: and many other such like things ye do. And he said unto them, Full well ye reject the commandment of God, that ye may keep your own tradition."** And so as you can see, the Bible does warn us about observing traditions, because most Christian traditions are rooted in paganism, you know the worshipping of idols. And the interesting thing is, the early Christians did not celebrate Jesus's birth, because they considered the celebration of anyone's birth to be a pagan custom. I mean it's crazy, but it seems like Christianity instead of destroying the pagan traditions, it seems like Christianity pretty much adopted a whole lot of the pagan traditions. And this is why the Catholic church seems to have a whole bunch of traditions that it observes as part of their doctrine, and it's because the Catholic church is pretty much the earliest modern church, you know, it's the church that pretty church promoted Christianity as the world religion, and so not only does it bare responsibility for shaping how we pretty much worship God (as in Sunday service), it also bares the responsibility for promoting all the pagan traditions that it allowed to become part of our worship of God and Christ, as in Christmas.

And so yeah, December 25th is not even a holy day, it's pretty much an idol worship day that was adopted as the day to celebrate the birth of Christ. And the funny thing is, most scholars believe that the birth of Christ is actually not even in the month of December at all, they believe that the birth of Christ most likely happened between March and September, with September being the most likeliest (when the weather was still warm enough for the shepherds to still be able to tend to their flocks outside, even at night), as we read in the book of Luke 2:8-11 (KJV); **"And there were in the same country shepherds abiding in the field, keeping watch over their flock by night. And, lo, the angel of the Lord came upon them, and the glory of the Lord shone round about them: and they were sore afraid. And the angel said unto them, Fear not: for, behold, I bring you good tidings of great joy, which shall be to all people. For unto you is born this day in the city of David a Saviour, which is Christ the Lord."** And so as you can see, the birth of Christ seems to have pretty much happened when the weather was warm, evidenced by the shepherds being able to tend to their flocks even at night.

And so anyway, yeah, December 25th definitely makes Christmas to be an unholy celebration, because we can't celebrate the birth of Christ using a tradition that is not holy, you know, because God demands that anything we present to Him should be holy, you know, anything we present to Him should be pure, and Christmas is not pure, because December 25th is not pure, it's pretty much almost idolatry, you know what I mean? And December 25th is not the only thing that makes Christmas not holy, the Christmas tree also makes Christmas unholy. And the interesting thing is, the Bible actually kinda talks about the Christmas tree. I mean, the Bible doesn't call it the Christmas tree, but it does talk about how they cut down trees and decorate them and worship them. Hold on, let me see if I can find the verse, because I do remember reading it a while back, so hold on, let me find it. Ok, alright, I found the verse, check this verse out and tell me if it doesn't sound like the Bible is talking about the Christmas tree (indirectly). KJV-Jeremiah 10:1-4; **"Hear ye the word which the**

LORD speaketh unto you, O house of Israel: Thus saith the LORD, Learn not the way of the heathen, and be not dismayed at the signs of heaven; for the heathen are dismayed at them. For the customs of the people *are* **vain: for** *one* **cutteth a tree out of the forest, the work of the hands of the workman, with the axe. They deck it with silver and with gold; they fasten it with nails and with hammers, that it move not."** Ok, so what do you think, doesn't this verse seem to implicate the Christmas tree? And did you notice how it said, **Thus saith the LORD, Learn not the way of the heathen.** And what that means is, we should not be using the customs of the unbelievers, in this case the pagans. And that is what we have done with our celebrating of Christmas, we have used the custom of the pagans in our desire to celebrate the birth of Christ. I mean it's crazy, but almost everything about Christmas was directly adopted from the pagan customs, you know, like the December 25th day (which was the concluding day of the pagan winter festival called "the Saturnalia, which they observed as the birth of their sun-god Mithras), and the Christmas tree (which they decorated and worshiped as their idol god), and even to the Mistletoe (which the pagans believed it had mystical powers.

    I mean, come on, really, are we really gonna take the pagan idol customs and apply them to Christianity? I mean, wow, it is very amazing at what and or how we just allow anything to be part and or symbols of holiness, you know what I mean? I mean it's like we love to test God, you know, it's like we want to tell God how we gonna worship and or celebrate Him, you know, no matter what He thinks and or no matter how He would prefer for us to worship and or celebrate Him, you know what I mean? And the reason why I say this is because, to think that these so called Christian traditions that are not Biblical at all to have survived and be practiced for centuries is to really not understand what being a Christian is all about, you know, it really shows how lost we really are as Christians. And the reason why I say this is because, if we really understood what being a Christian is all about, we would know that we can't just present to God anything that is not holy, you know, we can't just present to God stuff that we think God will like and or take joy in thinking that we had good intensions in doing so, because to God, if the root of it is evil, then the fruit of it is evil, you know, something that has an evil spirit in it, then the fruit of it will have part of the evil spirit in it, you know what I mean? And so, we can't just take a tradition that has idol worship in it and use that for our holy purposes and think God will accept that offering, you know, just because we had good intentions with our usage of it. I mean, no, it does not work like that, we can't present tainted stuff to God, the Bible has so many verses about this, you know, the Bible has so many verses that talk about whatever we present to God to make sure that it is not unclean, you know, and Christmas is so unclean that we Christians should not be celebrating it, because in doing so it's like we telling God that we gonna celebrate the birth of our Lord and Savior using this idol pagan custom and if you don't like it oh well, we gonna do it anyway. I mean, is that crazy or not? And to think that we have been doing it for centuries is really disheartening, you know, it's really sad. And the reason why it's sad is because, a lot of people don't really know that they are actually not celebrating Christ at all during Christmas time, you know, a lot of people actually don't know that Christmas is not really a holy holiday, you know, millions of people don't actually know that they are continuing the pagan traditions of celebrating the sun-god Mithras on December 25th and they are continuing the pagan traditions of cutting down trees and decorating them and worshipping them, you know what I mean? I mean, is that crazy or not? I mean, just think about it, just think about how many millions of Christians each year buy trees (because nowadays the Christmas trees are already cut and available to purchase, including also the fake trees that come in a box and all you have to do is reassemble them) and take them to their houses and decorate them and put a mistletoe on top of them, I mean, wow, millions of people are placing idols in their homes without even knowing it, man, God help us, we are truly lost!

And so anyway, yeah, Christmas is not a holy holiday, we have pretty much been bamboozled, you know, we have pretty much been deceived. And who you might asked has bamboozled and or deceived us, well, it's that old serpent the devil, you know, the one that tricked Adam and Eve into sinning, well, he is still doing it, you know, he has been tricking us for centuries and he is still tricking us even today, you know, because that is the only way that this gruesome mistake of Christmas could have survived up to this day without even much of a challenge from Christians who are supposed to be Godly, you know, from Christians who are supposed to really know about the Bible and the ways of the Lord, you know, from Christians who are supposed to be the light of the world, you know, from Christians who are supposed to have the Holy Ghost in them. I mean, are you understanding what I'm trying to say here? And what I'm trying to say is, if we truly say we are Christians, and if we truly believe that we are saved, and if we truly believe that we have the Holy Ghost in us, then there's no reason why we can't and or should not be able to see the truth of the Bible and gain the wisdom to understand how God wants us to not only live our lives here on earth, but also understand how God wants us to worship Him (which is in truth and with a pure heart). And then so, if we are truly Christians, and if we are truly saved, and if we truly have the Holy Ghost in us, then there's no reason why we can't gain the wisdom and strength to correct our errors, from traditions, doctrines, and etc., that we find to be unbiblical, because not doing so is like we telling God that we don't care what He thinks, we gonna do it our way and He can like it or not, or He can accept it or not, but we have made up our minds, and that's it, take it or leave it, you know, it's like we dictating to God how we gonna worship Him instead of how He wants us to worship Him. And this scenario has the devil's hands all over it, you know, because the devil knows how to trick us, I mean he's been doing it for centuries, you know, so he is pretty good at it, you know what I mean? But, we are children of God, we are descendants of Abraham, Moses, David, and other prophets that God highly favored, and most importantly we are followers of Jesus Christ our Lord and Savior, and so there's no reason that the devil should be able to deceive us so easily, and there's no reason that we can't correct the parts of our Christianity that the devil has caused to be corrupted for so long (centuries), I mean there's no reason for it, there's no reason for us to remain idle when we know the truth and have the ability and or tool (the Bible) to correct our mistakes, you know, so we and the next generations to come can practice our Christianity not only in truth, but also with a pure heart, you know, so God can truly be pleased with our worship and praising of Him!

And so yeah, Christmas is not a holy holiday, and we as Christians have no business celebrating it. I mean, I know that we mean well in our celebrating Christmas, you know, I know that in our hearts we want to celebrate the birth of our Lord and Savior Jesus Christ, I mean, on the surface, if Christmas wasn't so tainted, if it wasn't taken from the pagan customs, we could probably been able to celebrate it with no problem, but, as we can see, that is not the case, you know, Christmas is not pure, you know, Christmas is very unclean, and so we just gonna have to let it go, you know, we just gonna have to stop celebrating it, because in doing so all we will be doing is continuing with the pagan idol worshipping customs, which totally goes against the Bible's teaching of how we should worship God. And so I know it's gonna be very very hard for most people to give up Christmas (and this is one of the reasons why it has continuing for centuries, you know, because people have a hard time giving it up, and so chose to just hope that God will see their intentions, which is still wrong), but as the Bible says, when we grow up we give up childish things, so here to, when we become grown-ups in spiritual growth, we must also give up things that we practiced when we did not know better (childish in spirit).

And so yeah, it's gonna be hard to give up Christmas, I myself will have a hard time giving up Christmas, you know, because I have pretty much been observing it all my life, you know, from when I was younger till now (at 42 years old). And so yeah, I'm really gonna miss Christmas, I mean, I miss it already, lol! And the funny thing is, I'm writing about this (ending Christmas) during Christmas time, you know, so I'm really in my feeling right about now, you know, it's almost like I'm saying goodbye to Christmas as I'm watching others celebrate it. And so yeah, it's gonna be hard to give up Christmas, but that is just exactly what I have to do, especially if I want to become a better Christian, which is what I'm aiming for, and that is one of the reasons why I decided to write this book, you know, so I can force myself to really get into the Bible and learn what being a Christian really means, and by doing so, not only can I work on implementing what I learn so I can become a better Christian, but also so

I can share what I learn so we can all work on becoming better Christians, you know, which is what God wants us to do, you know, become better Christians! But yeah, it's gonna be hard to give up Christmas, and what's gonna make it even harder is having to explain to your kids and other kids in your family why you can't buy them Christmas presents (because Christmas presents carry the spirit of Christmas, so that has to stop too), but kids are more willing to understand and give you a pass, especially if they love the Lord. But who you gonna have a harder time explaining to why you don't celebrate Christmas anymore is the adults in your family (your extended family), the adults are the ones who gonna give you a hard time about it, you know, they are the ones who gonna look at you like you crazy, you know, they are the ones who gonna blame you for either ruining Christmas for them, as they reason that you are just being an overzealous Christian. But, you just gonna have to deal with it, because truth is truth and over time some of your family members will either join you in not celebrating Christmas or they will just have to accept your stance on it, but either way, as long as you are honest with them and try to show them the truth, it doesn't matter what they think or act towards you, because at the end of the day, it's God who you really want to please, you know what I mean? And as for your children, you could probably do as I did on Christmas day, which is, I bought them their favorite snacks (for my daughter it was a big bag of hot fries, for my older son it was a big thing of chocolate chip cookies, and for my younger son it was 2 big sprinkles doughnuts) and some sodas (we don't really do sodas in our house), and they enjoyed it. But it was a little bit easier for my kids to accept not getting presents, because my wife's church doesn't celebrate Christmas, so they kind of grow up knowing that not every Christian celebrates Christmas and or gets presents. It was a little bit harder for our younger son to understand why he couldn't even get presents, but my wife re-explained it to him and he seemed to be cool with it. But I probably was the one who had a harder time with not getting our kids and the other kids in our family presents, you know, because even though my wife's church didn't celebrate Christmas, we still bought presents for our kids and the other kids in our extended family, you know what I mean? And the thing is, even though we didn't do Christmas at our house (for almost the last 18 years), you know, no Christmas tree or decorations, we did do Christmas at my dad's house, you know, my kids grandfather's place. Yeah, my dad's place is where we did Christmas at every year, and so even though we didn't do Christmas at our house, our kids and me and my wife (my wife had already kinda given up Christmas a long time ago but not me, that's why we didn't do it at our house) still got to celebrate Christmas by going to my dad's place (where there was a Christmas tree and nice decorations and the sound of Christmas music, you know, the whole thing) and open the presents and enjoy a big Christmas feast with the rest of our family members.

And so yeah, we still got a chance to celebrate Christmas every year by going to my dad's house, but, not this year, you know, because not only did I finally come to really understand and accept that Christmas was actually not a holy day, it just so happened that my dad was not having the traditional Christmas gathering at his house this year (for personal family reasons), which worked perfect for me, because I was really having a hard time decided whether to go or not, and whether to buy presents for the kids in the family or not, you know, in my attempt to not participate in Christmas anyone. And so when my dad said we can't do Christmas this year, I was really relieved, you know, because that would mean not only would I not have to make the decision whether to go or not (which I most likely would have ended up going, but I would not have not bought any presents, you know, so I wouldn't be actively participating), but it would mean that I could actually start my not celebrating Christmas anymore cold turkey, you know, without participating in any part of it. It was kind of hard not to wish people Merry Christmas, but at least I could say happy holidays, you know, but it was still kind of weird. But, that's what we did on Christmas day, you know, my kids ate their favorite snacks, my wife watched some T.V. and took some naps, and I spent most of the day on the computer typing working on this book, and I was actually working on the chapter about homosexuality on Christmas day, lol!

And so yeah, it's gonna be hard to give up Christmas, but that is what we must do in order to be right in the eyes of God, you know, that is what we must do if we really want to be better Christians, you know, because as the Bible says; Mark 7:7-9 (KJV); **"Howbeit in vain do they worship me, teaching *for* doctrines the commandments of men. For laying aside the commandment of God, ye hold the tradition of men, *as* the washing of pots and cups: and many other such like things ye do. And he said unto them, Full well ye reject the commandment of God, that ye may keep your own tradition."**

EASTER

Easter is calculated as the first Sunday after the first full moon on or after the March equinox, which can fall anywhere between March 22nd and April 25th. An equinox is an astronomical event in which the plane of Earth's equator passes through the center of the sun, which occurs twice a year, around March 20 and September 23. The March equinox is used to mark the beginning of spring. On the day of the equinox, night and day are about the same length, and what that means is, night time (darkness) lasts as long as day time (sunlight).

Now, here is the story of how we got Easter, and it goes something like this: when Queen Semiramis (also known as Ashtoreth, and later known as the fertility goddess Astarte or Ishtar) husband died (King Nimrod, the king of Babylon, later known as the pagan idol god Baal), she got pregnant and had a son (Tammuz) whom she said was conceived immaculately (supernaturally) and whom she claimed to be her husband King Nimrod resurrected, whom she also claimed to be the promised Messiah and should be worshipped as a god. And this story is why a lot of critics who don't believe in the virgin birth of Jesus Christ like to say that Christians got the idea of not only the virgin birth but also the idea of Christ's resurrection from the pagans, you know, and it's because of this story, the pagan origin of Easter, you know, about birth, death and resurrection. But the thing is, the coming of Christ (the Messiah) was already prophesied about even before Queen Ashtoreth (later known as the fertility goddess Ishtar or Eostre) gave the myth of King Nimrod being resurrected as her son Tammuz. And so in actuality the pagans knew about the prophesy of the coming Messiah and when Queen Ashtoreth convinced them that her son was that Messiah, they went ahead and ran with the story and the story became very popular. But the Bible does say that false Messiahs are gonna pop up, so we can pretty much regard Tammuz as one of them. But the people did believe in the deception, so much so that they not only started worshipping Tammuz as a god, but they also started celebrating his so called resurrection, and of course used the name of his mother (whom they considered a fertility goddess) Eostre as the name for their resurrection celebration. And do you notice how Easter just happens to be celebrated in the spring time, do you know why that is? And it's because in the spring that is when most vegetation seem to spring out (no pun intended) from the ground, you know, that's when vegetation seem to come back to life, you know what I mean? I mean it's like, most vegetation tend to die out in the winter, but then when spring time comes, most vegetation tend to come back to life, you know, so it's like they are being reborn, and or it's like they are being resurrected, you know what I mean? And so this is why the pagans chose spring time to celebrate the resurrection of their idol god Tammuz, and it's because that is the time of the year that life seems to be reborn, as with the vegetation.

And so yes ladies and gentlemen, we pretty much got our Easter celebration thing from the pagans, I mean, even down to the Easter bunny and the decorating of eggs (which I will let you do the research on those yourself and see what a mess of a custom the Easter bunny and decorating of eggs is), it's all pretty much a pagan tradition that we are celebrating every spring time. I mean, man, it never fails, I mean it's almost like we like to be deceived, doesn't it? I mean it's crazy, but yes my fellow Christians, yes it seems like once again we have been bamboozled, you know, it seems like once again we have been utterly deceived. I mean, wow, how does it happen, I mean, why do we keep allowing the devil to trick us over and over and over again!? I mean, come on, when are we gonna say enough is enough, you know, when are we gonna put our feet down and say, hey look here you devil, we are tired of you deceiving us and are not gonna take it anymore, you know what I mean? Because I mean, how long are we gonna continue to practice traditions that are not Biblical. I mean, when are we gonna stand up and say if it is not Biblical then it's got to go, you know what I mean? I mean, I don't know about you, but I definitely cannot just go through the motions and pretend that ignorance is bliss, you know, because in this case ignorance is definitely not bliss, you know what I mean?

Now, I do understand that a lot of people truly don't know that there are a lot of pagan traditions in Christianity (as a whole), and the reason why they don't know is because most people are very passive when it comes to religion you know, most people just don't take the time to investigate and or to do research on what it is they are being taught about their religion and or faith, you know what I mean? And what I mean is, most people just take it at face value that their leaders and or pastors pretty much know a lot more about their faith than they personally could ever understand and or could ever learn on their own, you know, most people just accept what is being taught to them about their faith and just follow like sheep. And this is why you have a lot of people practicing doctrines and or traditions that are not Biblical at all, and it's because they accept being ignorant, and therefore just follow any leader and or pastor, you know, hoping and or trusting that their pastors not only have their best interest at heart, but they hoping and trusting that their pastors are teaching them real truths from the Bible.

And so anyway, yeah, we Christians pretty much got our Easter celebration from the pagans, because not only is it not in the Bible, but the time of the year and the name we call the celebration is all from the pagans. And the funny thing is, the resurrection of Christ was actually nowhere near spring time, it was actually most likely in the middle of winter in January, with January 17th being the most likely date of Jesus's resurrection. And the other funny thing is, it's most likely that Christ's resurrection didn't even happen on a Sunday, it most likely happened on a Saturday. I mean, wow, how the heck did we totally disregard January (where there is actually Biblical evidence for it) and end up settling on March or April (when the first full moon happens after the March equinox) to celebrate what could be argued as the most important act that Jesus did as our Savior, which was to defeat death (by His resurrection) so we could gain salvation through His victory, you know what I mean?

Now, you are probably wondering where is the evidence that January is most likely the month that Jesus was crucified, died, buried and resurrected. And you are probably wondering where is the evidence that on a Saturday is most likely the day of the week that Jesus resurrected than on a Sunday. Well my friends, well my fellow Christians, the evidence is in the Bible, the Bible actually has this date in plain sight, but somehow it seems like no one has really paid much attention to it, because if they did, we could have probably been correctly this mistake a long time ago, you know what I mean? Ok, so, here is the evidence, and it's kind of tricky, but I'm gonna try my best to explain it to you as simply as I can (with the verses), so you can see it and examine it for yourself, so you won't have to take my word for it.

Ok, alright, let's do it, let's check out some verses that will give us the evidence of Jesus's resurrection being in January and being on a Saturday instead of a Sunday. Ok so, before we check out some verses let's see what we already know first (common knowledge), and what we know is that; Jesus was betrayed (the night of the last super) and was captured, the next day He was tried, crucified, and buried, the day after that, His tomb was reinforced and two watch man were put in place to guard it, then the third day He rose again (resurrected). And what else do we know, we know that Mary Magdalene came early Sunday morning (first day of the week) to check on the tomb. Ok, so now that we have these basic facts in mind, let's check out some verses and see if they will tell us when Jesus was most likely crucified, buried and resurrected.

Ok, so the first verse we gonna start with is, Matthew 26:2 (KJV); **"Ye know that after two days is *the feast of* the passover, and the Son of man is betrayed to be crucified."** So what we learn from this verse is that, Jesus is gonna be betrayed on the day of the Passover (which is when the last super also happened). Let's continue: Matthew 26:17-21; **"Now the first *day* of the *feast of* unleavened bread the disciples came to Jesus, saying unto him, Where wilt thou that we prepare for thee to eat the passover? 18 And he said, Go into the city to such a man, and say unto him, The Master saith, My time is at hand; I will keep the passover** at thy house with my disciples. <u>19</u> And the disciples did as Jesus had appointed them; and they made ready the passover. <u>20</u> Now when the even was come, he sat down with the twelve. <u>21</u> And as they did eat, he said, Verily I say unto you, that one of you shall betray me."

Matthew 26:31; "Then saith Jesus unto them, All ye shall be offended because of me this night: for it is written, I will smite the shepherd, and the sheep of the flock shall be scattered abroad."

Matthew 26:36; "Then cometh Jesus with them unto a place called Gethsemane, and saith unto the disciples, Sit ye here, while I go and pray yonder."

Matthew 26:45-50; "Then cometh he to his disciples, and saith unto them, Sleep on now, and take *your* rest: behold, the hour is at hand, and the Son of man is betrayed into the hands of sinners.

<u>46</u> Rise, let us be going: behold, he is at hand that doth betray me.

<u>47</u> And while he yet spake, lo, Judas, one of the twelve, came, and with him a great multitude with swords and staves, from the chief priests and elders of the people.

<u>48</u> Now he that betrayed him gave them a sign, saying, Whomsoever I shall kiss, that same is he: hold him fast.

<u>49</u> And forthwith he came to Jesus, and said, Hail, master; and kissed him.

<u>50</u> And Jesus said unto him, Friend, wherefore art thou come? Then came they, and laid hands on Jesus, and took him." Ok, so Jesus finally got betrayed and the soldiers came and took Him, and this is still the night of the Passover. Let's continue reading:

Matthew 26:51-75; "And, behold, one of them which were with Jesus stretched out *his* hand, and drew his sword, and struck a servant of the high priest's, and smote off his ear.

52 Then said Jesus unto him, Put up again thy sword into his place: for all they that take the sword shall perish with the sword.

53 Thinkest thou that I cannot now pray to my Father, and he shall presently give me more than twelve legions of angels?

54 But how then shall the scriptures be fulfilled, that thus it must be?

55 In that same hour said Jesus to the multitudes, Are ye come out as against a thief with swords and staves for to take me? I sat daily with you teaching in the temple, and ye laid no hold on me.

56 But all this was done, that the scriptures of the prophets might be fulfilled. Then all the disciples forsook him, and fled.

57 And they that had laid hold on Jesus led *him* away to Caiaphas the high priest, where the scribes and the elders were assembled.

58 But Peter followed him afar off unto the high priest's palace, and went in, and sat with the servants, to see the end.

59 Now the chief priests, and elders, and all the council, sought false witness against Jesus, to put him to death;

60 But found none: yea, though many false witnesses came, *yet* found they none. At the last came two false witnesses,

61 And said, This *fellow* said, I am able to destroy the temple of God, and to build it in three days.

62 And the high priest arose, and said unto him, Answerest thou nothing? what *is it which* these witness against thee?

63 But Jesus held his peace. And the high priest answered and said unto him, I adjure thee by the living God, that thou tell us whether thou be the Christ, the Son of God.

64 Jesus saith unto him, Thou hast said: nevertheless I say unto you, Hereafter shall ye see the Son of man sitting on the right hand of power, and coming in the clouds of heaven.

65 Then the high priest rent his clothes, saying, He hath spoken blasphemy; what further need have we of witnesses? behold, now ye have heard his blasphemy.

66 What think ye? They answered and said, He is guilty of death.

67 Then did they spit in his face, and buffeted him; and others smote *him* with the palms of their hands,

68 Saying, Prophesy unto us, thou Christ, Who is he that smote thee?

69 Now Peter sat without in the palace: and a damsel came unto him, saying, Thou also wast with Jesus of Galilee.

70 But he denied before *them* all, saying, I know not what thou sayest.

71 And when he was gone out into the porch, another *maid* saw him, and said unto them that were there, This *fellow* was also with Jesus of Nazareth.

72 And again he denied with an oath, I do not know the man.

73 And after a while came unto *him* they that stood by, and said to Peter, Surely thou also art *one* of them; for thy speech bewrayeth thee.

74 Then began he to curse and to swear, *saying*, I know not the man. And immediately the cock crew.

75 And Peter remembered the word of Jesus, which said unto him, Before the cock crow, thou shalt deny me thrice. And he went out, and wept bitterly." Ok, so all this still happened the same night of the Passover. Let's continue reading:

Matthew 27:1-2; **"When the morning was come, all the chief priests and elders of the people took counsel against Jesus to put him to death: 2 And when they had bound him, they led *him* away, and delivered him to Pontius Pilate the governor."** Ok, so, we are now in the morning, and this morning does not mean the next day, no, the morning is still the same day, it's the morning of the same Passover day. Now, let me re-explain this, because I'm sure you are probably a little confused of what I'm saying about it being the morning of the same day. And the reason for my saying it is, you see, the Bible counts a day as being from evening to morning, you know, like from 6pm Wednesday to 6pm Thursday that would be considered as one day, in this case it would be a Wednesday. And then, 6pm Thursday to 6pm Friday would be considered the next day, you know, it would be Thursday. I know, I know it's kind of confusing, but you just have to play around with it a few times for it to really sink in, I mean, it really kicked my butt the first few times I tried to understand it, but it's not hard to understand, you just gotta play around with it a few times. You know what, let's check out a few verses that mention this, I think they will help you understand better.

Genesis 1:1-13 (KJV); **"In the beginning God created the heaven and the earth.**

2 And the earth was without form, and void; and darkness *was* upon the face of the deep. And the Spirit of God moved upon the face of the waters.

<u>3</u> And God said, Let there be light: and there was light.

<u>4</u> And God saw the light, that *it was* good: and God divided the light from the darkness.

<u>5</u> And God called the light Day, and the darkness he called Night. And the evening and the morning were the first day.

<u>6</u> And God said, Let there be a firmament in the midst of the waters, and let it divide the waters from the waters.

<u>7</u> And God made the firmament, and divided the waters which *were* under the firmament from the waters which *were* above the firmament: and it was so.

<u>8</u> And God called the firmament Heaven. And the evening and the morning were the second day.

<u>9</u> And God said, Let the waters under the heaven be gathered together unto one place, and let the dry *land* appear: and it was so.

<u>10</u> And God called the dry *land* Earth; and the gathering together of the waters called he Seas: and God saw that *it was* good.

<u>11</u> And God said, Let the earth bring forth grass, the herb yielding seed, *and* the fruit tree yielding fruit after his kind, whose seed *is* in itself, upon the earth: and it was so.

<u>12</u> And the earth brought forth grass, *and* herb yielding seed after his kind, and the tree yielding fruit, whose seed *was* in itself, after his kind: and God saw that *it was* good.

<u>13</u> And the evening and the morning were the third day." Ok, so, you see, a day in the Bible is from the evening to the morning, or we can say from sunset to sunset, which makes it twenty-four hours. So, do you

understand it a little bit better now, I hope so, because that is how we gonna calculate the three days that Jesus died to find out which day He resurrected. But for now let's get back to our story, when the morning had come and Jesus was taken to Pontius Pilate the governor.

Matthew 27:11-15; **"And Jesus stood before the governor: and the governor asked him, saying, Art thou the King of the Jews? And Jesus said unto him, Thou sayest.**

12 And when he was accused of the chief priests and elders, he answered nothing.

13 Then said Pilate unto him, Hearest thou not how many things they witness against thee?

14 And he answered him to never a word; insomuch that the governor marvelled greatly.

15 Now at *that* feast the governor was wont to release unto the people a prisoner, whom they would." Ok, notice how it says "at that feast", and the feast is the Passover, and as it was their custom on Passover they would release whatever prisoner the people wanted, and this time it was between Jesus and Barabbas, and of course the people chose Barabbas to be released. Let's continue reading:

Matthew 27:26-35; **"Then released he Barabbas unto them: and when he had scourged Jesus, he delivered *him* to be crucified.**

27 Then the soldiers of the governor took Jesus into the common hall, and gathered unto him the whole band *of soldiers*.

28 And they stripped him, and put on him a scarlet robe.

29 And when they had platted a crown of thorns, they put *it* upon his head, and a reed in his right hand: and they bowed the knee before him, and mocked him, saying, Hail, King of the Jews!

30 And they spit upon him, and took the reed, and smote him on the head.

31 And after that they had mocked him, they took the robe off from him, and put his own raiment on him, and led him away to crucify *him*.

32 And as they came out, they found a man of Cyrene, Simon by name: him they compelled to bear his cross.

33 And when they were come unto a place called Golgotha, that is to say, a place of a skull,

34 They gave him vinegar to drink mingled with gall: and when he had tasted *thereof*, he would not drink.

35 And they crucified him, and parted his garments, casting lots: that it might be fulfilled which was spoken by the prophet, They parted my garments among them, and upon my vesture did they cast lots." Ok, so this was still the Passover day when Jesus got crucified. Now, you probably wondering why I'm making you read all these verses instead of just giving you the date and day that is most likely the day Jesus resurrected, and the reason I'm showing you all these verses is so you can have a good picture in mind of how the whole crucifixion, death and resurrection unfolded, that way when we do the timeline to figure out the date and day of Jesus's resurrection you will be able to understand it better. Ok, alright, let's continue reading:

Matthew 27:45-50; **"Now from the sixth hour there was darkness over all the land unto the ninth hour.**

46 And about the ninth hour Jesus cried with a loud voice, saying, Eli, Eli, lama sabachthani? that is to say, My God, my God, why hast thou forsaken me?

47 Some of them that stood there, when they heard *that*, said, This *man* calleth for Elias.

48 And straightway one of them ran, and took a spunge, and filled *it* with vinegar, and put *it* on a reed, and gave him to drink.

49 The rest said, Let be, let us see whether Elias will come to save him.

50 Jesus, when he had cried again with a loud voice, yielded up the ghost."

Ok, so, as verse 50 says, Jesus yielded up the ghost, which means he finally died. And so as we can see, Jesus died on Passover day. And did you notice how on verse 46 it said, **"And about the ninth hour Jesus cred with a loud voice,"** well that pretty much tells us that Jesus pretty much died in the morning of the Passover day around 9am. Now, since we know that Jesus died on Passover, let's go find a verse or verses that tells us what month and day is the Passover, because once we find that, then we will have found the real month that Jesus died and resurrected, which will tell us when Easter should have really been celebrated, if it wasn't a pagan tradition, you know what I mean?

Ok, so, here it is my friends, here is that mysterious verse or better yet, here are the mysterious verses that have been hiding in plain sight that no one seem to have been able to find them, you know, the verses that are probably some of the most important verses in the Bible, you know, because not only do they tell us what month Passover took place, but they also let us know indirectly that this is also the month and day that Christ had died, you know what I mean? And so without further ado, here are the mysterious verses:

Exodus 12:1-18 (KJV); **"And the LORD spake unto Moses and Aaron in the land of Egypt, saying,**

2 This month *shall be* unto you the beginning of months: it *shall be* the first month of the year to you.

3 Speak ye unto all the congregation of Israel, saying, In the tenth *day* of this month they shall take to them every man a lamb, according to the house of *their* fathers, a lamb for an house:

4 And if the household be too little for the lamb, let him and his neighbour next unto his house take *it* according to the number of the souls; every man according to his eating shall make your count for the lamb.

5 Your lamb shall be without blemish, a male of the first year: ye shall take *it* out from the sheep, or from the goats:

6 And ye shall keep it up until the fourteenth day of the same month: and the whole assembly of the congregation of Israel shall kill it in the evening.

7 And they shall take of the blood, and strike *it* on the two side posts and on the upper door post of the houses, wherein they shall eat it.

8 And they shall eat the flesh in that night, roast with fire, and unleavened bread; *and* with bitter *herbs* they shall eat it.

9 Eat not of it raw, nor sodden at all with water, but roast *with* fire; his head with his legs, and with the purtenance thereof.

10 And ye shall let nothing of it remain until the morning; and that which remaineth of it until the morning ye shall burn with fire.

__11__ And thus shall ye eat it; *with* your loins girded, your shoes on your feet, and your staff in your hand; and ye shall eat it in haste: it *is* the LORD'S passover.

__12__ For I will pass through the land of Egypt this night, and will smite all the firstborn in the land of Egypt, both man and beast; and against all the gods of Egypt I will execute judgment: I *am* the LORD.

__13__ And the blood shall be to you for a token upon the houses where ye *are*: and when I see the blood, I will pass over you, and the plague shall not be upon you to destroy *you*, when I smite the land of Egypt.

__14__ And this day shall be unto you for a memorial; and ye shall keep it a feast to the LORD throughout your generations; ye shall keep it a feast by an ordinance for ever.

__15__ Seven days shall ye eat unleavened bread; even the first day ye shall put away leaven out of your houses: for whosoever eateth leavened bread from the first day until the seventh day, that soul shall be cut off from Israel.

__16__ And in the first day *there shall be* an holy convocation, and in the seventh day there shall be an holy convocation to you; no manner of work shall be done in them, save *that* which every man must eat, that only may be done of you.

__17__ And ye shall observe *the feast of* unleavened bread; for in this selfsame day have I brought your armies out of the land of Egypt: therefore shall ye observe this day in your generations by an ordinance for ever.

__18__ In the first *month*, on the fourteenth day of the month at even, ye shall eat unleavened bread, until the one and twentieth day of the month at even.

So, what do you think, did you see it, did you see the verses with the date and month on it. I mean, wow, there it is (verses 2, 6, &18), in plain sight, telling us not only what month and day Passover is on, but also letting us know what month and day Christ was crucified, died, buried and resurrected! So let's examine these verses a little bit more. Ok, let's start with the 2nd verse, and as you can see, the 2nd verse plainly tells us that the Passover is on the first month, and that is January, right!? And so right away we know that Christ pretty much died on January, because He died on Passover, right!? Ok, let's check out verse 6, and verse 6 says they should keep it until the 14th day of the same month, and the month is January, right!? Ok, let's check out verse 18, and verse 18 says; **In the first month, on the fourteenth day of the month at even, ye shall eat unleavened bread**, ok wow, did you see that, not only did it give the month, but it also gave the date, in the same verse! Man, I'm kind of speechless right about now, you know, because I'm kind of just having a hard time trying to think how could all these Christians who decided on celebrating Jesus resurrection on March or April just ignore these verses right here that plainly tell us that Jesus pretty much died and resurrected in January, you know what I mean?

And so anyway, yeah, Jesus died and resurrected in January, not March or April. And so now, since we know what date He died, let's see if we can figure out what date He resurrected. And figuring the date He resurrected shouldn't be that hard, because really all we have to do is count three days after the 14th, right!? And so here we go, 15, 16, 17, and there we go, we just figured out that Jesus died on the 17th of January around 9am. I mean, wow, how easy was that, that didn't take that much effort at all! And so now, since we now know the dates and month of Jesus's death and resurrection, let's see if we can figure out which day of the week that not only He was crucified and buried, but let's see if we can figure out what day of the week He had actually resurrected. Now, before we try to figure out the day of the week Jesus resurrected, let's go back and read the rest of the story of Jesus's crucifixion up to the part where Mary Magdalene went to check on the tomb and found it empty and the angel told her that Jesus had already resurrected and was on His was to Galilee. Ok, let's continue reading:

Matthew 27:51-66 (KJV); **"And, behold, the veil of the temple was rent in twain from the top to the bottom; and the earth did quake, and the rocks rent;**

52 And the graves were opened; and many bodies of the saints which slept arose,

53 And came out of the graves after his resurrection, and went into the holy city, and appeared unto many.

54 Now when the centurion, and they that were with him, watching Jesus, saw the earthquake, and those things that were done, they feared greatly, saying, Truly this was the Son of God.

55 And many women were there beholding afar off, which followed Jesus from Galilee, ministering unto him:

56 Among which was Mary Magdalene, and Mary the mother of James and Joses, and the mother of Zebedee's children.

57 When the even was come, there came a rich man of Arimathaea, named Joseph, who also himself was Jesus' disciple:

58 He went to Pilate, and begged the body of Jesus. Then Pilate commanded the body to be delivered.

59 And when Joseph had taken the body, he wrapped it in a clean linen cloth,

60 And laid it in his own new tomb, which he had hewn out in the rock: and he rolled a great stone to the door of the sepulchre, and departed.

__61__ And there was Mary Magdalene, and the other Mary, sitting over against the sepulchre.

__62__ Now the next day, that followed the day of the preparation, the chief priests and Pharisees came together unto Pilate,

__63__ Saying, Sir, we remember that that deceiver said, while he was yet alive, After three days I will rise again.

__64__ Command therefore that the sepulchre be made sure until the third day, lest his disciples come by night, and steal him away, and say unto the people, He is risen from the dead: so the last error shall be worse than the first.

__65__ Pilate said unto them, Ye have a watch: go your way, make *it* as sure as ye can.

__66__ So they went, and made the sepulchre sure, sealing the stone, and setting a watch."

Matthew 28:1-10; "In the end of the sabbath, as it began to dawn toward the first *day* of the week, came Mary Magdalene and the other Mary to see the sepulchre.

__2__ And, behold, there was a great earthquake: for the angel of the Lord descended from heaven, and came and rolled back the stone from the door, and sat upon it.

__3__ His countenance was like lightning, and his raiment white as snow:

__4__ And for fear of him the keepers did shake, and became as dead *men.*

5 And the angel answered and said unto the women, Fear not ye: for I know that ye seek Jesus, which was crucified.

6 He is not here: for he is risen, as he said. Come, see the place where the Lord lay.

7 And go quickly, and tell his disciples that he is risen from the dead; and, behold, he goeth before you into Galilee; there shall ye see him: lo, I have told you.

8 And they departed quickly from the sepulchre with fear and great joy; and did run to bring his disciples word.

9 And as they went to tell his disciples, behold, Jesus met them, saying, All hail. And they came and held him by the feet, and worshipped him.

10 Then said Jesus unto them, Be not afraid: go tell my brethren that they go into Galilee, and there shall they see me."

Ok, so, that was some good reading wasn't it, I mean it is so detailed you can pretty much almost picture it perfectly, right!? So anyway, let's go ahead and figure out which day of the week Jesus actually resurrected. Now, it's kind of tricky, but I'm gonna try to make it as simple as I can, so hopefully you won't be too confused. So, let's look at Matthew 28 verse 1, and it says; **"In the end of the sabbath, as it began to dawn toward the first *day* of the week, came Mary Magdalene and the other Mary to see the sepulchre."** Ok, so, did you see how it said, **In the end of the sabbath, as it began to dawn toward the first *day* of the week,** and what this tells us is that, they came just as the Sabbath was ending and just before the first day of the week had begun. And so, ladies and gentlemen let me ask you, based on this knowledge of them coming just before the first day of the week had begun, which day of the week must the resurrection of Jesus must have taken place? And so yes my friends, if you said the resurrection must have taken place on Saturday you are correct, you can go ahead and pat yourself on the back, because you my friend have just figured out which day of the week Jesus had really resurrected. I mean, was that not easy or what!? I mean, wow, man, the answer was just right there staring at us in plain sight, but as you can see, not many people's spiritual eyes are open, you know, that's why a lot of people who are supposed to be Bible scholars can't seem to figure this out, and we figured it out in no time at all. Now, truth be told, I just actually figured it out not that long ago as I'm typing this, because before that, the answer was not as clear to me before it just hit me, you know, as I re-read the verse, it just hit me, you know, It just occurred to me that Mary Magdalene and the other Mary actually came to the tomb when it wasn't actually the first day of the week yet, you know, it was just about to be the first day of the week. And wow, man, what a revelation, I mean, I thank God for letting me see the answer of Jesus's resurrection day so plainly, because before that, I was having a hard time thinking how I'm gonna explain it to you, you know, how I'm gonna make it simple enough for you to easily understand it. And so I thank God for showing me the answer in such a simple way, because otherwise I would have had to go through this whole method of counting backwards from Sunday until we get 72 hours (which is 3 days and would be a Wednesday) and then we would have had to double check it by counting back forward from Wednesday until we get 72 hours (which is 3 days and would be a Saturday and then I would have had to explain a few more details in between of why we are counting that way, which would have probably confused you a little, it not a lot. But, I thank God that I don't have to do all that, because God just revealed to us in plain sight that the women came just before it was the first day of the week, which is a much easier explanation then the one I was gonna present beforehand. So thank you Lord thank you Lord, for making my job here a lot easier on this one, and actually for making my job here easier on a lot of the issues that we have been covering in this Bible study that we have been doing, you know, because this is what this book is, it's a written Bible study, you know what I mean?

Ok, so, wow, man, is the Bible amazing or what, I mean, it pretty much has almost all the answers in plain sight, you know, it's just us who fail to search them out, you know what I mean!? But so anyway, let's review, what have we learned about Jesus's day of crucifixion and resurrection? We have learned that Jesus was pretty much crucified on the day of the Passover, which is on January 14th, and we have learned that He died around 9am Wednesday morning, and we have learned that He resurrected on Saturday January 17th at around 9am. Man, wow, I really don't know what to say right about now, I mean, I really having a hard time understanding why we are not celebrating Jesus's resurrection in January 17th, I mean, what do you think, isn't that crazy or what!? I mean, how do we straight out ignore what the Bible tells us is pretty much most likely the day of Jesus's resurrection but instead we decide to celebrate His resurrection in March or April. I mean, does that make any sense to you, because it truly doesn't make any sense to me?! I mean, why do we choose to be so ignorant? And actually I don't think it's really a matter of us being so ignorant, I think it's a matter of us choosing to be so disobedient to the word of God. And the reason why I say this is because, most Christian leaders (bishops, pastors, priests, preachers and so on), most of them pretty much know what the Bible actually says about a lot of issues that we practice incorrectly, you know, whether it be doctrine, traditions, customs or etc., you know, but instead of correcting them, a lot of church leaders act like they are blinded to the truth, which I would hate to believe it's the case, because if that is the case, then we are in even more of a bigger mess than what I thought we were in before I started writing this book. I mean, are you understanding what I trying to say here, and what I'm trying to say is, if our church leaders don't know what the heck they are talking about, that would mean we got millions and millions of Christians being led by so called men and women of God who don't even really understand the Bible themselves, you know, which is like the blind leading the blind, as the Bible likes to say. And so this is why I would like to think that most of our church leaders just choose not to challenge the system (their church and or their denominations), for whatever reason (mostly probably because they know it would be a monumental task, which could very possibly cause them to be alienated from their churches and or denominations).

I mean it's crazy, but for whatever reason we Christians are just so scared of challenging the system, you know, even if we truly know that the system is wrong, you know, even if we know that the system is corrupt, you know, even if we know that the system is wicked, you know, even if we know that the system is totally in disobedient to the word of God. I mean, I don't know what it is, I just don't get it, and I'm just really having a hard time understanding why we would just go along with false doctrines, you know, I'm just really having a hard time understanding why we would just go along with traditions that have no Biblical justifications for them. I mean, are you understanding what I'm trying to say here, and what I'm trying to say is, church leaders need to stand up and correct all these church practices that have no Biblical justifications for them, you know, church leaders need to stand up and correct all these un Biblically sound practices that do nothing but make millions of Christians disobey God's word ignorantly. I mean, man, we are in some serious spiritual trouble, us as Christians as a whole, you know, the body of Christ really needs some serious re-awakening, you know, we Christians really need to examine ourselves (as a whole) and really do some serious doctrinal reforms, you know, because otherwise we gonna continue to go through the motions of pretending that we are worshipping God but instead we are just playing holiness, you know what I mean?

Man, that's it, I'm done with this chapter, this chapter has just taught me that we Christians are really lost, you know, this chapter has just really opened my eyes to how so disobedient we Christians are to the word of God. I don't know, I'm just starting to feel a little depressed right about now. I don't know, it's hard to explain it, but my chest just started to feel a little extra heavy right about now. You know what, I think I know what it is, I think the reason why I'm feeling this way is because, I just can't help but think of how many people (Christians) in the world who are practicing their Christianity the way they have been taught and who observe all these false doctrines and traditions, I just can't help to think how they might be actually practicing their Christianity in vain, you know, worshipping and praising God in a manner that is not pleasing to God, you know, worshipping and praising God using false doctrines and or traditions. Man, there's a lot of work to be done, our church leaders have really let us down, and this is why I think the Bible says something like; **"many are called but few are chosen"**, and, **"the harvest is plenty but the laborers are few!"**

Anyway, that's it for this chapter, I hope it was very informative to you as it was to me, and let's pray that God will give us the strength to work to correct these issues (doctrines, traditions, etc.) that plague our Christian community, you know, so we and the next generations to come can worship and praise the Lord in truth and with a pure heart. Alright, cool, Amen!

9

FOLLOW ME

Hey ladies and gentlemen, guess what, we are finally at the last chapter of this marvelous Bible study we have been doing so far, and I think I have left the best chapter for last, because in this chapter we gonna hear from our Lord and Savior Jesus Christ himself, as we read the verses that He spoke himself when He was here on earth with us and see what He has to tell us about what it really means to be a Christian, you know, because after all, being a Christian means to be a follower of Christ, and so I can't think of any better way of learning about what it really means to be a Christian than from the words of Jesus himself, you know what I mean!? And so, alright, ok, let's get into the Bible and see what Jesus himself has to tell us about what being a Christian really means!

Matthew 4:17-25 (KJV); **From that time Jesus began to preach, and to say, "Repent: for the kingdom of heaven is at hand."**

18 And Jesus, walking by the sea of Galilee, saw two brethren, Simon called Peter, and Andrew his brother, casting a net into the sea: for they were fishers.

19 And he saith unto them, "Follow me, and I will make you fishers of men."

20 And they straightway left *their* nets, and followed him.

21 And going on from thence, he saw other two brethren, James *the son* of Zebedee, and John his brother, in a ship with Zebedee their father, mending their nets; and he called them.

22 And they immediately left the ship and their father, and followed him.

23 And Jesus went about all Galilee, teaching in their synagogues, and preaching the gospel of the kingdom, and healing all manner of sickness and all manner of disease among the people.

24 And his fame went throughout all Syria: and they brought unto him all sick people that were taken with divers diseases and torments, and those which were possessed with devils, and those which were lunatick, and those that had the palsy; and he healed them.

25 And there followed him great multitudes of people from Galilee, and *from* Decapolis, and *from* Jerusalem, and *from* Judaea, and *from* beyond Jordan."

Now, did you notice how when Jesus told those fishermen to follow him, did you notice how they just dropped everything they were doing and right away just started following Jesus, I mean, isn't that some great faith or what? And the reason why I say this is because, I mean, just think about it, there they were, minding their own business, living their lives, then out of nowhere a guy comes along and says, hey, follow me and I will make you fishers of man! I mean, think about that for a moment, how would you have reacted, would you have had the courage and or faith to drop everything, and or would you have had the faith to give up your normal livelihood and follow a stranger that you have just seen for the first time who out of nowhere came to you and said, hey, follow me and I will make you a fisher of men!? I mean, wasn't that great courage, and or, wasn't that great faith in their part! I mean, that whole scenario is just so amazing to me, but, that is what faith is all about, you know, faith is about having great courage to believe in something and or someone that you have never seen before, you know, faith is about trusting deep down in your heart that this person who is telling you to follow Him is really the Messiah, you know, faith is about accepting that the person who is telling you to follow Him is the true Lord and Savior, you know, faith is about truly believing that this person who is telling you to follow Him is indeed the son of God who will lead you closer to God, you know what I mean? And the thing about faith is, it's one of those things were you just feel it, you know, it's one of those things that your heart just tells you that this is it, you know, your heart just gives you the assurance that you are indeed putting your trust and belief in the right person, you know, your heart just gives you peace and comfort that you have indeed found the true Messiah who will lead you not only to know God, but who will lead you to be part of God's Kingdom, aka Heaven. And so, those fishermen had great faith that Jesus was indeed the Messiah that the prophets talked about, and so when Jesus came out of nowhere and said hey, follow me, they didn't hesitate for a second to drop whatever they were doing and followed Him. And this is also what Jesus is still telling us today, you know, He is still telling us to follow Him. But of course we can't follow Him literally like how His disciples did, you know, because He is not physically here with us on earth today, but we can still follow Him spiritually, you know, we can still follow Him by obeying and or living our lives the way He taught us from the examples and teachings He left us in the Bible, you know what I mean?

And so, the first lesson that we have just learned about being a Christian is that, our faith in Jesus should be without question, and with that, we should obey His teachings of how we should live our lives as His followers, because this is how we can spiritually follow him nowadays, you know, by His teachings in the Bible. Ok, alright, so let's continue reading and see what Jesus has to teach us about what it really means to be a Christian!

Matthew 5:1-48; **And seeing the multitudes, he went up into a mountain: and when he was set, his disciples came unto him:**

2 **And he opened his mouth, and taught them, saying,**

3 **Blessed** *are* **the poor in spirit: for theirs is the kingdom of heaven.**

4 **Blessed** *are* **they that mourn: for they shall be comforted.**

5 **Blessed** *are* **the meek: for they shall inherit the earth.**

6 **Blessed** *are* **they which do hunger and thirst after righteousness: for they shall be filled.** So, this verse is pretty much telling us that, blessed are those who are trying to be better Christians, and in doing so we shall be filled with the knowledge and understanding of what being a Christian is all about, and will be given the wisdom and strength to walk in righteousness.

7 **Blessed** *are* **the merciful: for they shall obtain mercy.**

8 **Blessed** *are* **the pure in heart: for they shall see God.**

9 **Blessed** *are* **the peacemakers: for they shall be called the children of God.**

10 **Blessed** *are* **they which are persecuted for righteousness' sake: for theirs is the kingdom of heaven.**

11 **Blessed are ye, when** *men* **shall revile you, and persecute** *you***, and shall say all manner of evil against you falsely, for my sake.** This is a strong verse right here, and it's telling us that, not to worry about people mistreating us, and or not to worry about people talking badly about us when we are out there working to spread the word of God and to teach them about Jesus Christ.

12 Rejoice, and be exceeding glad: for great *is* your reward in heaven: for so persecuted they the prophets which were before you. And this verse is telling us that we should rejoice in knowing that our reward is in heaven, so not to worry about being mistreated as we work to spread the word of God, because even the prophets who came before us were persecuted, so we shouldn't be shocked if we too get persecuted.

13 Ye are the salt of the earth: but if the salt have lost his savour, wherewith shall it be salted? it is thenceforth good for nothing, but to be cast out, and to be trodden under foot of men.

14 Ye are the light of the world. A city that is set on an hill cannot be hid.

15 Neither do men light a candle, and put it under a bushel, but on a candlestick; and it giveth light unto all that are in the house.

16 Let your light so shine before men, that they may see your good works, and glorify your Father which is in heaven.** Alright, this is a great verse right here, and it's telling us that we shouldn't be afraid to let our good works that we do for the Lord be known to the world, because in doing so, the world can know about the good works that Christians are doing in the world, which will cause the world to want to honor and glorify God.

17 Think not that I am come to destroy the law, or the prophets: I am not come to destroy, but to fulfil.

18 For verily I say unto you, Till heaven and earth pass, one jot or one tittle shall in no wise pass from the law, till all be fulfilled. Ok, in verses 17 and 18 Jesus is telling us that, He did not come to put an end to the Law (the Ten Commandments), but to fulfil them, which means, He came to help us gain favor in God's eyes through Him, as

He fulfil the Law on our behalf, because truth be told, if we had to do it on our own we couldn't, and God already knew this and that's why He brought us Jesus, you know, so Jesus could fulfil the Law on our behalf, you know, as He takes on our sins and pay for them on the cross. And so, even though we are no longer under the Law (meaning that our salvation is not based on the Law) but under Grace (meaning that our salvation is based on our accepting Jesus Christ as our Lord and Savior), it doesn't mean that we are no longer required to obey the Law (the Ten Commandments), no, we are still required to obey the Law. And this is why Jesus said on verse 18; **For verily I say unto you, Till heaven and earth pass, one jot or one tittle shall in no wise pass from the law, till all be fulfilled,** which means the Law still stands until the end of the world.

19 **Whosoever therefore shall break one of these least commandments, and shall teach men so, he shall be called the least in the kingdom of heaven: but whosoever shall do and teach *them*, the same shall be called great in the kingdom of heaven.**

20 **For I say unto you, That except your righteousness shall exceed the *righteousness* of the scribes and Pharisees, ye shall in no case enter into the kingdom of heaven.** Wow, the scribes and the Pharisees must have been really out of touch with the word of God huh, just doing their own thing, you know, pretending to be holy. And the scribes and the Pharisees were like the religious leaders of the Bible time, and so their influence on the people was great, and so they could easily mislead the people, and Jesus here is telling them that they should aim to be more righteous than the scribes and the Pharisees, because Jesus knows that the scribes and the Pharisees doctrine is pretty corrupt, like most of our churches nowadays.

21 **Ye have heard that it was said by them of old time, Thou shalt not kill; and whosoever shall kill shall be in danger of the judgment:**

22 But I say unto you, That whosoever is angry with his brother without a cause shall be in danger of the judgment: and whosoever shall say to his brother, Raca, shall be in danger of the council: but whosoever shall say, Thou fool, shall be in danger of hell fire.

23 Therefore if thou bring thy gift to the altar, and there rememberest that thy brother hath ought against thee;

24 Leave there thy gift before the altar, and go thy way; first be reconciled to thy brother, and then come and offer thy gift. So, in verses 22,23, and 24, Jesus is saying that you should make peace with your brother (and I think brother here means any individual that you may have issues with) before you go to the altar and give offering. And the reason why Jesus says this is because, God wants us to have a pure heart, you know, He wants us to have no malice toward anybody, and so this is why Jesus says we should go and make peace with the people that we might be having issues with before we come to Him with an offering. And sometimes this might be hard, because the person might have really done bad towards you, but, God still wants us to make peace with them, you know, so our hearts can be pure, you know, with no anger and or vengeance inside of us.

25 Agree with thine adversary quickly, whiles thou art in the way with him; lest at any time the adversary deliver thee to the judge, and the judge deliver thee to the officer, and thou be cast into prison. So, here also Jesus is saying that we should make peace as soon as possible with anybody we have problems with, that way the situation won't get even worse, and we end up in even a worse situation than before.

26 Verily I say unto thee, Thou shalt by no means come out thence, till thou hast paid the uttermost farthing.

27 Ye have heard that it was said by them of old time, Thou shalt not commit adultery:

28 **But I say unto you, That whosoever looketh on a woman to lust after her hath committed adultery with her already in his heart.** Ok, wow, what, we commit adultery just by looking and lusting after a woman!? Oh boy, I think a lot of us men are just gonna have to do a whole bunch of repenting on a daily or hourly basis, you know what I mean guys, especially in the summer time, lol. I mean, wow, Jesus is not playing around, just by looking we have committed adultery! You know what, I think we should pass a law to make all the women wear those outfits like the Muslim women wear, you know, the ones that cover them from head to toe, you know, so we men won't be able to see how sexy they are, so we won't have to look and lust after them, you know what I mean guys, lol. No, I'm serious, because that's pretty much the only way that most of us guys won't be able to commit adultery in our hearts, you know, because when we see a sexy woman, most of us guys can't help it but look and start to lust after them in our hearts, you know what mean? And our lusting after them is usually subconsciously, you know, it's like our nature to hunt comes calling as soon as we see a sexy woman and before we know it, we are lusting after them. And what usually happens is that we usually catch ourselves lusting after we have already did the lusting, usually within seconds of it, but lusting don't take that long to occur, usually within seconds of eye contact of them. And so anyway, sorry guys, I don't think the women are gonna agree with the wearing and covering of themselves from head to toe, and see we just gonna have to try our best not to lust after them, because we are already married individuals, so we just gonna have to learn and or we just gonna have to train our minds to not lust after the sexy women we see, you know, instead we could just appreciate their sexiness and turn away quickly and keep it moving, you know what I mean guys, lol. Hey, Jesus don't play around, He's standard for pureness is way, way, way, way higher than what we think of it. And this is why we definitely need Him in our lives, you know, so He can help us overcome some of our fleshly desires, you know what I mean!?

29 **And if thy right eye offend thee, pluck it out, and cast *it* from thee: for it is profitable for thee that one of thy members should perish, and not *that* thy whole body should be cast into hell.**

30 And if thy right hand offend thee, cut it off, and cast *it* from thee: for it is profitable for thee that one of thy members should perish, and not *that* thy whole body should be cast into hell.

31 It hath been said, Whosoever shall put away his wife, let him give her a writing of divorcement:

32 But I say unto you, That whosoever shall put away his wife, saving for the cause of fornication, causeth her to commit adultery: and whosoever shall marry her that is divorced committeth adultery. Wow, this verse right here, this verse right here, I'm speechless, wow! This verse is tough, Jesus is not playing around, no divorcing except in the case of fornication, otherwise it is considered as committing adultery. I mean, wow, we not even supposed to marry a person that has been divorced, that is considered adultery, wow! I mean, did you understand this verse, and what this means is that, when you get married, the person you are married to is considered your wife or husband till death do y'all apart, you know, that person is still considered (in the eyes of God) as being still your wife or husband even if the two of you are divorced, and so, if you get re-married, in the eyes of God it will be like you are cheating on your ex-wife or husband with this new person that you are married to, you know, because in the eyes of God your ex-wife or husband is still your wife or husband until one of you dies, you know what I mean? And so, this verse is very tough, because it leaves no room for divorcing and re-marrying at will, you know it only allows us to divorce if one of us cheats on the other person, and that's what fornication on this verse means, cheating (aka sexual immorality).

And so, wow, I wonder how many Christians are out there committing adultery with their second or third wives right now, you know what I mean!? And I wonder how many Christians have ever read this verse before, you know, because man, this verse is very tough on divorcing, and if a lot of Christians really took heed to this verse, there would be a lot less divorces happening in the world, because Christians contribute a lot to the number of divorces that happen each year, am I right or wrong? And so, sorry ladies and gentlemen, but as Christians were are not allowed to just divorce our wives or husbands for any reason, you know, we can't just divorce our spouses just because we can't stand their butts no more, you know, we can't just divorce our spouses just because we think we will be much happier with someone else (the grass is greener on the other side), or because we think we would rather be by ourselves than with the person we are married to, you know what I mean? And so this verse is very tough, because just imagine if you find yourself in an awful marriage, you know, a marriage where abuse and or other dysfunctions are routine, I mean, what are you to do then? And so, this verse is very tough, because there's not much room for a spouse to leave their wife or husband who might be extra trifling without risking committing adultery by divorcing their trifling spouse, you know what I mean? And the reason why I say this is because, most people who divorce eventually want to get re-married, but if they do so they will pretty much be committing adultery (according to this verse), you know, they will pretty much be committing adultery every time they make love to their new wife or husband, you know what I mean?

And so, man, this verse is very tough, but, that's the Bible for you, it demands very high standards, and it has very strict requirements for how we Christians should live our lives, you know, so we can be as righteous as we can be in the sight of God. But, as you already know, this verse is very hard for most Christians to uphold, because we as human beings we really desire happiness, and if we get caught up in a relationship that is causing us to be very unhappy, it becomes very hard to us to just stick to the relationship, especially if the other person doesn't even seem interested in trying to work to make it better (by going to marriage counseling and such). And so this verse can be very tough for most Christians to uphold, but we must try anyway, you know, because that is what Jesus demands of us. Man, being a Christian can be very tough sometimes, right, but hey, it is what it is, God knows our hearts, you know, He knows whether we are trying to obey the rules of the Bible or not, you know, He already knows our strengths and weaknesses, you know what I mean? And so, if you find yourself in a marriage that is not working, you know, if you find yourself in a marriage where your trifling spouse doesn't seem to want to work on the marriage to make it better, then you might just be left with no choice but to divorce their trifling butts, and then what you might have to do is just remain single (no dating at all) until your ex dies (however long that is), then you will be free to marry again. I mean, man, I don't really know what to tell you about how you can try to uphold this verse, if you find yourself in a bad marriage, where the other person is trifling without cheating on you, you know, because if they are being trifling and cheating at the same time, then you can divorce them with no problem, because it looks like the cheating is what breaks the bond of marriage between two people in God's eyes, you know what I mean? And so yeah, this can be a very tough verse to uphold, so hopefully if we find ourselves in a divorced and re-married situation, hopefully God will have mercy on us and forgive us for it, because God knows how miserable it can be to not only stay in a bad marriage, but I'm sure God knows how miserable it can be to have to wait until the ex-wife or husband dies (which can be a very very long time) before you can be free to marry again, you know what I mean?

And so yeah, this verse can prove to be very hard to uphold, so let's all just hope and pray that we find good spouses so we don't have to worry about facing the prospect of divorcement, because that would really suck, because most of us would most likely end up re-marrying, which would mean we are living in sin, you know, by committing adultery against our ex-wives or ex-husbands. Man, anyway, hey, take care of each other y'all, because God greatly treasures the institution of marriage, so let's pray that our marriages will be honorable to God, which means let's pray that our marriages will last to the end (till death do us part), you know, so we don't have to present to God new marriages that come from people who have been married before and their exes are still alive, you know what I mean, cool?!

33 Again, ye have heard that it hath been said by them of old time, Thou shalt not forswear thyself, but shalt perform unto the Lord thine oaths:

34 But I say unto you, Swear not at all; neither by heaven; for it is God's throne:

35 Nor by the earth; for it is his footstool: neither by Jerusalem; for it is the city of the great King.

36 Neither shalt thou swear by thy head, because thou canst not make one hair white or black.

37 But let your communication be, Yea, yea; Nay, nay: for whatsoever is more than these cometh of evil. Hey, it looks like verses 33-37 is telling us that we shouldn't swear or take an oath by using God's name in it, you know, we shouldn't take an oath by saying something like; "I swear to God" or other variations of it. I mean, wow, this is a very interesting verse, and I would be lying if I said I totally understand it, but I'm guessing that Jesus doesn't want us to involve God in our swearing, because to do so would be like to use God's name in vain I suppose, you know, especially since most times people tend not to keep or tell the truth in their swearing in the first place, you know what I mean?

38 Ye have heard that it hath been said, An eye for an eye, and a tooth for a tooth:

39 But I say unto you, That ye resist not evil: but whosoever shall smite thee on thy right cheek, turn to him the other also. Now, I don't think Jesus on this verse is literally telling us to turn and let whoever smacks or punches us on the right cheek to turn and let them punch us on the left cheek as well, no, I believe what Jesus is telling us here is that we should not retaliate and smack or punch them back, which is what most of us would do, right!? Because I mean, how many of us would actually just let someone punch us twice without us retaliating, not many of us, right? And so what Jesus is telling us here is really to be the bigger man (so to speak) and not to retaliate.

40 And if any man will sue thee at the law, and take away thy coat, let him have *thy* cloke also.

41 And whosoever shall compel thee to go a mile, go with him twain.

42 Give to him that asketh thee, and from him that would borrow of thee turn not thou away.

43 Ye have heard that it hath been said, Thou shalt love thy neighbour, and hate thine enemy.

44 But I say unto you, Love your enemies, bless them that curse you, do good to them that hate you, and pray for them which despitefully use you, and persecute you;

45 That ye may be the children of your Father which is in heaven: for he maketh his sun to rise on the evil and on the good, and sendeth rain on the just and on the unjust.

46 For if ye love them which love you, what reward have ye? do not even the publicans the same?

47 And if ye salute your brethren only, what do ye more *than others*? do not even the publicans so?

48 Be ye therefore perfect, even as your Father which is in heaven is perfect. So, verses 40-48 is pretty much telling us that we should be good to everybody, you know, we should be good to not only the people that love us, but we should also be good to even people who hate us, you know what I mean? And the reason why Jesus is telling us this is because He wants us to be good in the sight of God, and so in order to do that we should be good to everyone, friends or foe. And I mean, I know it's not so easy to love people that hate you, but as Christians we are called to be the light of the world, which means we are called to be a blessing to the world, which means we are called to show goodness to the world, and so, by showing love to even our enemies, the world will come to regard Christians as a blessing in the world, which will do nothing but bring honor to God and may even cause the world to want to know more about our Lord and Savior Jesus Christ. Ok, let's continue reading and see what more Jesus has to teach us about what it really means to be a Christian!

Matthew 6:1-34 (KJV); **Take heed that ye do not your alms before men, to be seen of them: otherwise ye have no reward of your Father which is in heaven.**

2 Therefore when thou doest *thine* alms, do not sound a trumpet before thee, as the hypocrites do in the synagogues and in the streets, that they may have glory of men. Verily I say unto you, They have their reward.

3 But when thou doest alms, let not thy left hand know what thy right hand doeth:

4 That thine alms may be in secret: and thy Father which seeth in secret himself shall reward thee openly. Ok, so, what verses 1-4 mean is that, when you do your good deeds don't do them for showing off so you can get praises from people, but instead just do them humbly without making it such a big deal.

5 And when thou prayest, thou shalt not be as the hypocrites *are*: for they love to pray standing in the synagogues and in the corners of the streets, that they may be seen of men. Verily I say unto you, They have their reward.

6 But thou, when thou prayest, enter into thy closet, and when thou hast shut thy door, pray to thy Father which is in secret; and thy Father which seeth in secret shall reward thee openly.

7 But when ye pray, use not vain repetitions, as the heathen *do*: for they think that they shall be heard for their much speaking.

8 Be not ye therefore like unto them: for your Father knoweth what things ye have need of, before ye ask him. Ok, what verses 5-8 are telling us is that, we should not be trying to show off how well we ca pray, you know, we shouldn't use our ability to be able to pray well as a way to show people how holly we really are, but instead we should humbly pray in private, you know, because God already knows what we need before we even ask Him.

9 After this manner therefore pray ye: Our Father which art in heaven, Hallowed be thy name.

10 Thy kingdom come. Thy will be done in earth, as *it is* in heaven.

11 Give us this day our daily bread.

12 And forgive us our debts, as we forgive our debtors.

13 And lead us not into temptation, but deliver us from evil: For thine is the kingdom, and the power, and the glory, for ever. Amen.

14 For if ye forgive men their trespasses, your heavenly Father will also forgive you:

15 But if ye forgive not men their trespasses, neither will your Father forgive your trespasses.

16 Moreover when ye fast, be not, as the hypocrites, of a sad countenance: for they disfigure their faces, that they may appear unto men to fast. Verily I say unto you, They have their reward.

17 But thou, when thou fastest, anoint thine head, and wash thy face;

18 That thou appear not unto men to fast, but unto thy Father which is in secret: and thy Father, which seeth in secret, shall reward thee

openly. Ok, in verses 16-18 Jesus is telling us that when we are fasting, we shouldn't make it a big deal to where we want everyone to know that we are fasting, but instead we should humbly fast, you know, make it a private thing.

19 Lay not up for yourselves treasures upon earth, where moth and rust doth corrupt, and where thieves break through and steal:

20 But lay up for yourselves treasures in heaven, where neither moth nor rust doth corrupt, and where thieves do not break through nor steal:

21 For where your treasure is, there will your heart be also. In verses 19-21, Jesus is telling us that our focus should not be in being rich here on earth, but our focus should be in being rich up there in Heaven. And these verses are also telling us that, were our focus is, that is where our hearts will be. And so it's like, if we are rich here on earth, then our hearts and minds will be focused on our riches here on earth, but if we are rich in Heaven (spiritually), then our hearts and minds will be focused on our riches in Heaven (which means we will not be consumed by the things of this world, but focused on growing closer to God).

22 The light of the body is the eye: if therefore thine eye be single, thy whole body shall be full of light.

23 But if thine eye be evil, thy whole body shall be full of darkness. If therefore the light that is in thee be darkness, how great *is* that darkness!

24 No man can serve two masters: for either he will hate the one, and love the other; or else he will hold to the one, and despise the other. Ye cannot serve God and mammon. What Jesus is telling us on this verse is that, we cannot serve two masters, which means, we cannot serve God and money (or treasures) equally, one will suffer or be short changed.

And what this means is that, if our focus is on gaining lots of money, then it will be hard to focus on serving God when we are too busy chasing money, you know what I mean? And so, even though there's nothing wrong with wanting to be prosperous, we have to be careful not to make money our main focus in our lives, because in doing so will mean we have made money as our master, because we gonna spend more time thinking about gaining money instead of thinking about serving God.

25 Therefore I say unto you, Take no thought for your life, what ye shall eat, or what ye shall drink; nor yet for your body, what ye shall put on. Is not the life more than meat, and the body than raiment?

26 Behold the fowls of the air: for they sow not, neither do they reap, nor gather into barns; yet your heavenly Father feedeth them. Are ye not much better than they?

27 Which of you by taking thought can add one cubit unto his stature?

28 And why take ye thought for raiment? Consider the lilies of the field, how they grow; they toil not, neither do they spin:

29 And yet I say unto you, That even Solomon in all his glory was not arrayed like one of these.

30 Wherefore, if God so clothe the grass of the field, which to day is, and to morrow is cast into the oven, *shall he* not much more *clothe* you, O ye of little faith?

31 Therefore take no thought, saying, What shall we eat? or, What shall we drink? or, Wherewithal shall we be clothed?

32 (For after all these things do the Gentiles seek:) for your heavenly Father knoweth that ye have need of all these things.

33 But seek ye first the kingdom of God, and his righteousness; and all these things shall be added unto you.

34 Take therefore no thought for the morrow: for the morrow shall take thought for the things of itself. Sufficient unto the day *is* the evil thereof. Ok, so, in verses 25-34, Jesus is telling us that we shouldn't worry so much about our lives here on earth, because God already knows what we need, and so we should first work to attain salvation and be righteous, then God will provide for what we need here on earth. Now, of course we still need to get a job and work hard to maintain a living, but we shouldn't let that get in the way of us working to be better Christians, as Jesus is teaching us how!

Matthew 7:1-29 (KJV); **Judge not, that ye be not judged.**

2 For with what judgment ye judge, ye shall be judged: and with what measure ye mete, it shall be measured to you again.

3 And why beholdest thou the mote that is in thy brother's eye, but considerest not the beam that is in thine own eye?

4 Or how wilt thou say to thy brother, Let me pull out the mote out of thine eye; and, behold, a beam *is* in thine own eye?

5 Thou hypocrite, first cast out the beam out of thine own eye; and then shalt thou see clearly to cast out the mote out of thy brother's eye. Ok, what Jesus is telling us in verses 1-5 is that, before we go out and try to fix other people's problems and or sins, we should first work to fix our own problems and or sins, then we will be clean enough to try to fix and or help other people with their problems and or sins.

6 Give not that which is holy unto the dogs, neither cast ye your pearls before swine, lest they trample them under their feet, and turn again and rend you. Now, this is an interesting verse, I don't totally understand it, but I believe it means that we should not waist our time trying to share the gospel with people who don't really have any interest in hearing it, you know, we shouldn't waist our time trying to share the truth of the gospel with people who are stuck and or stubborn in their ways, you know, something like that. But if you have a different meaning to this verse please email me so I can check it out.

7 Ask, and it shall be given you; seek, and ye shall find; knock, and it shall be opened unto you:

8 For every one that asketh receiveth; and he that seeketh findeth; and to him that knocketh it shall be opened. In verses 7 and 8, Jesus is telling us that if we seek we shall find it, and if we knock it shall be opened, and if we ask we shall receive it. And guess what, that is exactly what we are doing in this book, you know, we are asking, knocking, and seeking for the truth of the Bible, and I have to confess, I am receiving, the Bible is being opened to me, and I am finding the truth that I've been seeking, and I hope you are too.

9 Or what man is there of you, whom if his son ask bread, will he give him a stone?

10 Or if he ask a fish, will he give him a serpent?

11 If ye then, being evil, know how to give good gifts unto your children, how much more shall your Father which is in heaven give good things to them that ask him? Ok, so, in verses 9-11 Jesus is telling us that we can ask for specific things and God will give them to us. Now, most people think that this means we can ask for things like, houses, cars, jobs, money, or etc, you know, mostly material things, but in actuality Jesus is not even talking about material things, He's pretty much talking about things like, strength, health, wisdom, comfort, peace, favor, faith, salvation, you know, things like that. And I mean, God already knows what we need on a daily basis anyway (as far as sustenance is concerned), you know, so we don't need to worry so much about that, because if our faith is real, then we are all good, God will make a way for us to survive, you know, God will provide, you know what I mean?

12 Therefore all things whatsoever ye would that men should do to you, do ye even so to them: for this is the law and the prophets. So this verse pretty much means that we should treat others like how we would like to be treated.

13 Enter ye in at the strait gate: for wide *is* the gate, and broad *is* the way, that leadeth to destruction, and many there be which go in thereat:

14 Because strait *is* the gate, and narrow *is* the way, which leadeth unto life, and few there be that find it. So verses 13 and 14 is telling us that it is easier for us to live a lifestyle that will lead us to Hell than to live a lifestyle that will lead us to Heaven. And that's why it says that it's gonna be a few that find the narrow gate that leads to life but the gate that leads to destruction is straight and wide, and most people are gonna go into that one.

15 Beware of false prophets, which come to you in sheep's clothing, but inwardly they are ravening wolves.

16 Ye shall know them by their fruits. Do men gather grapes of thorns, or figs of thistles?

17 Even so every good tree bringeth forth good fruit; but a corrupt tree bringeth forth evil fruit.

18 A good tree cannot bring forth evil fruit, neither *can* a corrupt tree bring forth good fruit.

19 Every tree that bringeth not forth good fruit is hewn down, and cast into the fire.

20 Wherefore by their fruits ye shall know them. In verses 15-20 Jesus is telling us that we should look out and or be aware of false prophets (preachers and such), who come to us looking holy on the outside, but in the inside are nothing but deceivers. And He also tells us that we will know them by their fruits (which means by their doctrines), and if their fruits are corrupt (which means if their doctrines are corrupt), then they are pretty much false prophets (which means they are false preachers). And this is one of the reasons why we are so lost as Christians, and it's because we are following so many false prophets (aka preachers), you know, it's almost like we love to be lied to, you know, it's almost like we love to be taken advantage of, you know what I mean? I mean it's crazy, but the reason why these false prophets continue in their deceptive ways is because we Christians as so gullible, you know, we are so easy to fool, you know what I mean? I mean it's crazy, but I see it all the time, millions of Christians being fooled to pay their little money to a fake ministry that promises them a huge money return from God, you know, because that little money that the poor Christian was able to send in (because a lot of these false prophets tend to advertise on television about their power to pray for people to gain prosperity and such things like that) is supposed to be an investment (sowing seed) which will grant them a huge return from God. I mean, come on man, really, are we Christians really just gonna fall for that, because to do so is not to understand what God is all about, which is your soul, you know, your salvation, and it don't matter whether you live in a mention or whether you live in a mud house, God cares more about your salvation and not your earthly living condition. And I mean sure, God can give you favor if He chooses to for you to be prosperous here on earth, but that is at His own time and purpose, mostly so you can have the resources to help spread the gospel, not so you can live lavishly. And this is why every time I hear preachers say something like, "it's your season" or, "you better claim it", or "that new car is your", or "sow your seed today", or "when praises go up, blessings come down", and so on, when I hear these phrases I just shake my head, because this means that the congregation thinks that God is like Santa Clause, you know, all you gotta do is make a with and all these gifts will just suddenly appear out of nowhere, you know, they think that God will just grant them with stuff without they having to work hard for it, you know what I mean? I mean it's crazy, and this is why Jesus is telling us that we need to beware of false prophets, and we can know them by their fruits (aka doctrines). And so this is why some of us who are learning the real truth about God, Jesus and the Bible need to start speaking a lot louder so we can try and counter these false prophets that are out there deceiving our fellow Christians who for whatever reason find themselves in bondage to these false prophets who do nothing but take spiritual advantage (to gain money) instead of benefiting these Christians spiritually.

21 Not every one that saith unto me, Lord, Lord, shall enter into the kingdom of heaven; but he that doeth the will of my Father which is in heaven.

22 Many will say to me in that day, Lord, Lord, have we not prophesied in thy name? and in thy name have cast out devils? and in thy name done many wonderful works?

23 And then will I profess unto them, I never knew you: depart from me, ye that work iniquity. Wow, verses 21-23 are very interesting, I mean, did you see how Jesus said that not everyone that says "Lord, Lord" will enter into Heaven. And did you see how He said that many will say "have we not prophesied (which pretty much means to teach), and cast out devils, and done many wonderful works in thy name", and notice how He will say to them (on judgement day), "I never knew you, depart from me, ye that work iniquity." Wow, man, there's gonna be a lot of people who thought they were going to Heaven who are gonna be very disappointed. And the reason why Jesus said those verses is because, there's a lot of Christians who believe they are practicing Christianity the right way, you know, there's a lot of Christians who believe their doctrines are correct but they are not, you know, there's a lot of Christians who are practicing false doctrines but for whatever reason they refuse to correct them, and so they go ahead and worship and praise God using their false and or corrupt doctrine thinking that all is good, you know, they feel comfortable in their doctrine and truly believe that they are serving God, but in actuality they are pretty much just serving themselves, you know, in actuality they are just making themselves feel spiritually good, but in God's eyes they are worshipping and praising Him in vain, you know, because God does not accept anything that is not pure (sound doctrine). And so it's like, when judgement day comes, Jesus will have to tell a lot of Christians, hey sorry, but I never knew you. Man, that is gonna be terrible, right! And so this is why we need to wake up a whole lot of Christians who are just going through the motion and practicing their Christianity without examining whether what they are being taught is sound doctrine or not, you know, we need to sound the alarm that there are a lot of false prophets out there who are no good for them, you know, we need to tell them that there's a lot of preachers out there who are nothing but wolves in sheep clothing, you know what I mean?

24 Therefore whosoever heareth these sayings of mine, and doeth them, I will liken him unto a wise man, which built his house upon a rock:

25 And the rain descended, and the floods came, and the winds blew, and beat upon that house; and it fell not: for it was founded upon a rock.

26 And every one that heareth these sayings of mine, and doeth them not, shall be likened unto a foolish man, which built his house upon the sand:

27 And the rain descended, and the floods came, and the winds blew, and beat upon that house; and it fell: and great was the fall of it. So, in verses 24-27 Jesus is telling us that we need to be wise and trust on Him, as He is the rock that we should build our faith on, and not doing so is to be foolish.

28 And it came to pass, when Jesus had ended these sayings, the people were astonished at his doctrine:

29 For he taught them as *one* having authority, and not as the scribes.

Matthew 15:1-15 (KJV); **Then came to Jesus scribes and Pharisees, which were of Jerusalem, saying,**

2 Why do thy disciples transgress the tradition of the elders? for they wash not their hands when they eat bread.

3 But he answered and said unto them, Why do ye also transgress the commandment of God by your tradition?

4 For God commanded, saying, Honour thy father and mother: and, He that curseth father or mother, let him die the death.

5 But ye say, Whosoever shall say to *his* father or *his* mother, *It is* a gift, by whatsoever thou mightest be profited by me;

6 And honour not his father or his mother, *he shall be free*. Thus have ye made the commandment of God of none effect by your tradition.

7 *Ye* hypocrites, well did Esaias prophesy of you, saying,

8 This people draweth nigh unto me with their mouth, and honoureth me with *their* lips; but their heart is far from me.

9 But in vain they do worship me, teaching *for* doctrines the commandments of men.

10 And he called the multitude, and said unto them, Hear, and understand:

11 Not that which goeth into the mouth defileth a man; but that which cometh out of the mouth, this defileth a man.

12 Then came his disciples, and said unto him, Knowest thou that the Pharisees were offended, after they heard this saying?

13 But he answered and said, Every plant, which my heavenly Father hath not planted, shall be rooted up.

14 Let them alone: they be blind leaders of the blind. And if the blind lead the blind, both shall fall into the ditch. So, in verses 1-14 Jesus is telling us why are we transgressing God's commandments with our traditions, you know, why are we ignoring God's commandments and instead teach for doctrine our traditions, you know what I mean? And what I mean is (for example); we ignore observing the Passover (which is on January 14th), but instead we celebrate Easter (which is a pagan tradition) around March or April, and, we ignore observing the Sabbath (which is Saturdays), but instead we rest and worship God on Sundays (which is a pagan tradition), and, God commands us not to make images of Him or Jesus, but instead we continue to draw and or carve out statues that are supposed to be Jesus, which are totally false. And there's a bunch of other traditions that the churches hold to be Biblical but they are not, but those traditions are so ingrained in the churches doctrines that the churches refuse to correct them, and thereby they end up worshipping God in vain, you know, because God does not accept worship that is corrupt in any part, you know, like how Jesus says, if one part is corrupt, then the whole thing is corrupt, you know, so therefore for a doctrine to be pure, then the corrupt part has to be taken out (removed) so the whole can be pure, which then can be presented to God, you know what I mean?

Hey, did you notice what Jesus said on verse 14, He said: **Let them alone: they be blind leaders of the blind. And if the blind lead the blind, both shall fall into the ditch.** Wow, did you see that, no really, did you hear what Jesus just said, did you understand it!? And the reason why I'm saying this is because, there's a lot of Christians who are members of churches that have very corrupted doctrines, which means the church leaders don't really understand what the Bible is really teaching us, you know, there's a lot of church leaders who don't themselves really comprehend what being a Christians is really all about, and so they are teaching falsehoods and their congregations are accepting them as gospels, you know what I mean? I mean it's crazy, and this is why Jesus says, hey, just leave them alone, you know if they don't want to learn and or hear the truth, just leave them alone, you know, because they choose to be led by leaders who are blind to the truth, and so therefore, **both shall fall into the ditch.** Ok, so, wow, let's continue reading and see what else Jesus has to teach us about what it really means to be a Christian!

Matthew 16:21-28 (KJV); **From that time forth began Jesus to shew unto his disciples, how that he must go unto Jerusalem, and suffer many things of the elders and chief priests and scribes, and be killed, and be raised again the third day.**

<u>22</u> Then Peter took him, and began to rebuke him, saying, Be it far from thee, Lord: this shall not be unto thee.

<u>23</u> But he turned, and said unto Peter, Get thee behind me, Satan: thou art an offence unto me: for thou savourest not the things that be of God, but those that be of men.

<u>24</u> Then said Jesus unto his disciples, If any *man* will come after me, let him deny himself, and take up his cross, and follow me.

<u>25</u> For whosoever will save his life shall lose it: and whosoever will lose his life for my sake shall find it.

<u>26</u> For what is a man profited, if he shall gain the whole world, and lose his own soul? or what shall a man give in exchange for his soul?

<u>27</u> For the Son of man shall come in the glory of his Father with his angels; and then he shall reward every man according to his works.

28 Verily I say unto you, There be some standing here, which shall not taste of death, till they see the Son of man coming in his kingdom. So, in verse 23-28 Jesus is telling us that, as Christians we should not be desiring the things of this world, but we should desire to do the will of God, which means, however or whatever God puts in our hearts to do that will bring Him glory, and or whatever God puts in our hearts to do that will benefit the body of Christ (aka church, ministry, charity, missions, etc), that is where our focus should be, not on acquiring and or not on desiring worldly things, you know, like material things and or riches, you know what I mean? And I mean, there's nothing wrong with wanting to be prosperous, but your desire for prosperity should not be so you can afford a lifestyle of the rich and famous, no, your desire for prosperity should be so you can have the ability to support and or finance the cost of spreading the word of God to all nations, you know what I mean? And the reason why I say this is because, not everyone is called to be a preacher and or a pastor, you know, and so there's numerous ways that Christians can work to spread the word of God, and giving financial support to churches and or ministries that are set up with missions of various kinds that work to spread the word of God is one of the best ways that Christians can do good deeds indirectly around the world, you know what I mean? Because I mean, truth be told, not all of us have what it really takes to be a preacher and or a pastor (which means we are not called to it, but a lot of people force themselves into it, which is why the church community is in such terrible condition nowadays, and it's because we got a whole lot of people who don't really understand what being a preacher and or pastor is all about), but there are a lot of other ways we can contribute to the body of Christ, which is what all of us Christians are called to do (in some capacity) as best we can. And this my friends is a huge part of what being a Christian is all about, you know, contributing to the body of Christ by helping in spreading the gospel.

Now, notice how in verse 24 Jesus says: **If any *man* will come after me, let him deny himself, and take up his cross, and follow me.** And what Jesus means by this is that, if we want to be followers of Him (and that's what being a Christian means, a follower of Christ), then we have to deny ourselves, which means instead of living for this world, we instead live for the world to come (Heaven). Now, of course we are gonna still have to part of this world, but we shouldn't desire the things of this world, you know, like materialism and stuff like that. But yes, we still gonna have to have a job (9-5), and we still gonna have to have a house to live in, and we still gonna have to have a car to drive (transportation), and we can still go on vacations (to rest our minds and bodies), and we can still buy clothes (so we are not walking around naked, lol), you know, we can still do regular stuff like that, but we shouldn't get so caught up in living our earthly lives that we neglect and or that we forget what our real mission as Christians really is, which is to contribute the best we can to the body of Christ, therefor there is where our focus needs to be, not in our earthly lives, because as Jesus says, our earthly lives are only for a short season, but our Heavenly lives are forever.

And Jesus also says that we need to take up our crosses and follow Him, and what He means by this is that, as His followers we gonna face some hardships, we gonna face some burdens, we gonna face some mistreatments, and we gonna face many other unpleasant situations and or obstacles that the world is gonna throw our way as we work to spread the word of God, and those hardships, burdens, mistreatments, unpleasant situations, obstacles, and more, those are the crosses that we gonna have to carry with us as we follow Him (what you think, am I right or wrong on this verse, send me an email and let me know what you think about my explanation on this, because this just came to me right now as I'm writing). And so this is a huge part of what being a Christians is all about, you know, sacrificing our earthly lives for the life to come up in Heaven, and as we do so, we work to be the light of the world, you know, by doing good deeds in the world that will bring honor and glory to God. And so as you can see, being a Christian is not really a passive spirituality, you know, being a Christian is not just about being baptized, accepting Christ as your Lord and Savior, going to church on the regular, and or reading the Bible on the regular, no, being a Christian actually means more than that, you know, being a Christian actually involves us having to be active in contributing to the body of Christ by working to spread the word of

God, you know what I mean? And this is why on verse 27 Jesus says: **For the Son of man shall come in the glory of his Father with his angels; and then he shall reward every man according to his works.** And so you see, we are all called to contribute to the body of Christ, and we can do this in many various ways (missions, charity, time, money, etc.), as best as we can. And so yes my fellow Christians, being a Christian is not as easy as just accepting Christ as your Lord and Savior, getting baptized and going to church on the regular and paying tithe, no, there's a lot more to being a Christian than that, and that's why we need to really learn what it really means to be a Christian, which not many churches teach, and that may be because not many churches actually understand it themselves, you know, a lot of churches just go through the motions of routine doctrinal indoctrination, which does nothing but reinforce the churches doctrine (whether that doctrine is real or false) but leaves the church members ignorant to what it really means to be a Christian. And the reason why I say this is because, there are thousands and thousands of churches in the world, but the world is still in such a terrible shape, you know, the world is still becoming more and more wicked than holy, you know what I mean? And the reason why that is, is because even though we have thousands and thousands of churches out there, and even though we have over a billion Christians out there, the churches are not doing a good job of teaching all these Christians what it really means to be a Christian, and therefore even though we have over a billion Christians in the world, the world still don't see the blessing and glory of God shining through us Christians. And the reason why that is it's because we Christians don't really understand the blessing that God has already given us, and therefore we fail to let that blessing shine to the world through us, as we are supposed to do, you know, because as Jesus said, we are supposed to be the light of the world, but, if we ourselves don't understand what that means, then how can we let our light shine to the world. And this is why we have not been able to be that light in the world as Jesus says we are, and it's because we have not really grasped what being the light in the world really means. And I mean, we sing the songs all the time about how blessed and how we are the light of the world, but we have failed to really let that light come out of us and really shine to the world. I mean, are you understanding what I'm trying to say here, and what I'm trying to say is, if we Christians really understood what it really meant to be followers of Christ, then this world wouldn't be in such a terrible shape as it is today. And what I mean by this is that, if we Christians really did what the Bible calls us to do as followers of Christ, then there's no reason that there should be this much misery and suffering on this earth today, not with all these resources, and not with all this technology, and not with all these riches, and not with all these churches, and not with all this man power that we have as Christians in this world today. And what I mean by all this is that, there's no reason that the world should be suffering from so much hunger, and there's no reason that the world should be suffering from so much war, and there's no reason that the world should be suffering from so much curable diseases, and there's no reason that the world should be suffering from so much shortages of clean drinking water, and so on and so on, you know what I mean? And the reason why I say this is because, I truly believe that if we Christians, if just us Christians (without including people of other religions) did what it really meant to be a Christian, you know, I mean, if we Christians actually practiced our Christianity the way that Jesus wants us to practice it, I truly believe not only would the world be a better place, but I truly believe that more and more people of other religions would strongly consider becoming Christians themselves, because not only would they see the fruits of our labor in Christ, but they would be curious to want to find out about God and about our Lord and Savior whom we graciously serve, day in and day out. I mean, what do you think, I'm I right or wrong? No really, I want to know your opinion on this, so email me and let me know. And I mean, I know that there's always gonna be wars, and stuff like that, until the end of the world comes, but it doesn't have to be this bad, because the reason for most of these wars is over resources, you know, most wars break out because groups of people want to control areas of land that have the most resources, you know, because where the resources are, that's where the opportunity for wealth lays. And this is why most of Africa used to be colonized, and it's because there's a lot of resources in the continent, and that's why up to this day there seems to be so many unrest in a lot of countries in Africa, and it's because various groups can't decide how to share those resources, therefore they become ready to take up arms and go to war with each other instead of making peace and learn how to share those resources with each other.

And so anyway, back to us Christians, I truly believe that if we Christians really understood what it meant to be a Christian we could really help this world be a better place for all. And the reason why I say this is because, us Christians as a whole control a big part of the world's resources, you know, us Christians actually are a very wealthy community as a whole, you know what I mean? And so just imagine how much good we could actually do in the world if we actually decided to live up to what Jesus commands of us. I mean, are you understanding what I'm trying to say here? And what I'm trying to say is, instead of us Christians (as a whole) go out and spend our resources and or money foolishly and or selfishly on vanity (like mansions, yachts, fancy overpriced cars, fancy overpriced shoes and clothing, fancy overpriced jewelry, and so on and so on) that is not necessary, imagine how much good works we could really do in the world that not only would make life a lot more manageable for a lot of people in the world, but imagine how much honor and glory that would bring to God and our Lord and Savior Jesus Christ. I mean, are you understanding what I'm trying to say here, because this is what being a Christian really means, you know, doing good works in the world so not only can the world benefit from our good works, but so the good works can be a testament to our faith as followers of Christ. Are you starting to understand it a little bit better now, I sure hope so, because this is the best that I know how to explain what being a Christian is all about, and it's about being selfless, you know, it's about being each other's brothers and sisters in the Lord. And what that means is, we are called to look out for one another, you know, instead of caring for just me, myself and I, or instead of just caring about me and my family, Jesus commands us to care for all humanity, you know, to care for even our enemies. I mean, I don't know what else to tell you, but being a Christian doesn't just mean accepting Christ as our Savior, it doesn't mean just going to church on the regular, it doesn't mean just reading the Bible on the regular, no, it means to deny ourselves the things of this world (such as materialism and such) and to instead focus on building a more spiritual life, that involves contributing to the body of Christ our good works, as we await the return of our Lord and Savior Jesus Christ.

Alright, ok, so, guess what my friends, that's it, I think we are done with this Bible study that we have been doing here, I mean, wow, yeah, I think I'm done, I think I have said all that was in my heart to say, and I think we have done a good job of searching out the scriptures! I mean, what do you think, did you enjoy the reading, did you get much out of reading this book as I did writing it? I hope you did, because it was really a tour de force, you know, writing this book has really been an intense Biblical awakening for me. I mean, I knew it was gonna be kind of a challenge writing this book, but God had put it in my heart to write it since about five years ago, but I kept procrastinating on it year after year, but toward the end of last year (August 2016), God made it clear that I need to stop playing around and go ahead and write this book. And how He made it clear is by removing every excuse that I would use to postpone writing it (being too busy was the main excuse), by around August I suddenly found myself without any projects or any other little stuff that made me use as an excuse. And so it just hit me, you know what, I think God purposely removed all these distractions so I couldn't use them as an excuse to once again postpone the writing of this book. And the funny thing is, I actually felt ready to write this book, you know, I actually had no trepidations about whether I was qualified to write this book or not, you know what I mean? And so I went ahead and told my wife that I'm about to actually start writing this book, and with almost everything I do, once I make up my mind to do something, I go hard on it till it's done, and that's exactly what I did with the writing of this book, you know, lots of sleepless nights. But you know what, I am very happy with the outcome, you know, I'm very happy with how it turned out, because I wasn't one hundred percent sure if I had it in me to actually be able to discern the scriptures like I was able to do so. But, as the Bible says, with God anything is possible. And so I'm very great full that God opened my spiritual eyes and ears (which I prayed about), because that made the discerning of the scriptures actually very easy, I mean, the meanings of the verses were just revealing themselves to me just like that, I mean, sometimes I just had to take a few seconds to pray and thank God for the revelations. Man, I don't know what else to tell you, but I really want to thank you for picking up this book, I really hope it will be a positive influence in your life. And please, please share the book with as many people as you can, because that is why I wrote it, so we can all gain some wisdom, you know, so we can all try to really understand what being a Christian is really all about. So, I want to thank you again, and please, please feel free to email me (Christianitylost@gmail.com) with any questions, concerns, or whatever else is on your mind concerning this book and or concerning Christianity. Ok, that's it, may the Lord bless us all as we strive to be better Christians, and let the church say, Amen!!!

www.ingramcontent.com/pod-product-compliance
Lightning Source LLC
Chambersburg PA
CBHW061639040426
42446CB00010B/1490